AMERICAN HEROES

OF THE
20th Century

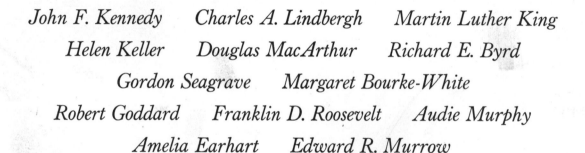

John F. Kennedy   Charles A. Lindbergh   Martin Luther King

Helen Keller   Douglas MacArthur   Richard E. Byrd

Gordon Seagrave   Margaret Bourke-White

Robert Goddard   Franklin D. Roosevelt   Audie Murphy

Amelia Earhart   Edward R. Murrow

William J. Donovan   Carrie Chapman Catt

Jonas Salk   Alan Shepard   Ernie Pyle

Marian Anderson   Dwight D. Eisenhower

AMERICAN HEROES

OF THE

20th Century

BY HAROLD and DORIS FABER

Illustrated with photographs

RANDOM HOUSE · NEW YORK

For helpful suggestions in the preparation of this book, the authors and the publisher are grateful to: Dr. Saul Benison and The National Foundation; Major H. Brady, U.S. Army Information Office; Commander Richard E. Byrd, Jr., and Miss G. F. Wood; Mrs. Woodrow Donovan, Curator of Manuscripts, Schlesinger Library, Radcliffe College; Mrs. Elizabeth O. Garvais, Public Education Division, American Foundation for the Blind; Paul Greenfeder, chief of the editorial library, The New York Times; Daniel Leab, History Department, Columbia University; and David C. McClure and Colonel Red Reeder.

Quotations from *Brave Men* by Ernie Pyle (copyright 1943, 1944 by Scripps-Howard Newspaper Alliance) are reprinted by permission of Holt, Rinehart and Winston, Inc. Several lines are quoted from *Life of a Burma Surgeon* by Gordon Seagrave by permission of W. W. Norton & Company, Inc. Passages in the chapter about Audie Murphy are based on and quoted from *To Hell and Back* by Audie Murphy (copyright 1949 by Audie Murphy), reprinted by permission of Holt, Rinehart and Winston, Inc.

PHOTOGRAPH CREDITS: American Foundation for the Blind, 30, 32, 34, 35; American Institute of Aeronautics and Astronautics, 12, 17, 100; Brown Brothers, 128, 132; Office of Admiral Byrd, Boston, 46, 51 (© 1926 National Geographic Society), 55; Cornell Capa, Magnum, 2; Columbia Broadcasting System, 108, 111, 112, 115; Commissaire Général d'Information et Propagande, Paris, 99 (top); Mrs. William J. Donovan, 116; Dwight D. Eisenhower Library, 169, 172; Alfred Eisenstaedt, Life Magazine © Time Inc., 73; Esther C. Goddard, 74 (© National Geographic Society), 76, 77, 78, 79, 80, 82; Oscar Graubner, © Time Inc., 69; Ernst Haas, Magnum, 20; C. M. Hayes & Co., Detroit (courtesy American Foundation for the Blind), 28; Bob Henriques, Magnum, 26; Hurok Attractions, 158, 163, 164, 165; Imperial War Museum, London, 110; Lockheed Aircraft, 105; Look Magazine, 160; NASA, 142, 144, 145, 147, 149; The National Foundation, 134, 137, 139, 140; New-York Historical Society, 130; Homer Paige, 64; Milton J. Pike, 150; Franklin D. Roosevelt Memorial Library, 87, 89; Schlesinger Library, Radcliffe College, 33, 124, 126, 127; © Time Inc., 66, 71; United Press International, 4, 5, 9, 10, 25, 27, 53, 86, 153, 155, 156; U.S. Army, 36, 38, 40, 41, 42, 118, 121, 154, 157, 166, 174; U.S. Information Agency, 114; U.S. Navy, 6; Universal Pictures Co., Inc., 92, 94, 97, 99 (bottom); Wide World Photos, 15, 18, 22, 44, 56, 58, 60, 61, 63, 70, 84, 91, 103, 106, 107, 119, 123.
   COVER: Dwight D. Eisenhower: Wayne Miller, Magnum; John F. Kennedy: U.S. Army; Franklin D. Roosevelt: Pictorial Parade; Alan Shepard: NASA.

CONTENTS

FOREWORD

Courage was the quality that President Kennedy most admired. After his death, his brother Robert said:

"He sought out those people who had demonstrated in some way, whether it was on a battlefield or a baseball diamond, in a speech or fighting for a cause, that they had courage, that they would stand up, that they could be counted on."

In choosing the heroes whose lives are described on the pages that follow, we looked first for this quality that John F. Kennedy so admired. But many American men and women of the twentieth century have proved their courage, and it has not been easy to select just twenty.

We have tried to show how varied are the paths that can lead to heroism—in war and in peace, in exploring the unknown and in expanding the bounds of man's knowledge. Because this century has posed such awesome new problems, it has also opened new opportunities for heroic service, and we have attempted to show this, too.

Any reader with a personal list of heroes may find that our roster differs somewhat from his own. Partly this may be because we have purposely excluded the world of sports, for the careers of many athletic heroes have been covered in another book in this same series, *Great American Athletes of the 20th Century*. But if our list differs from yours, we hope you will still be pleased to make the acquaintance of some other brave men and brave women.

HAROLD FABER
DORIS FABER

JOHN F. KENNEDY
Profile in Courage

"One fellow was running for a touchdown and I made a flying tackle and landed him . . ."

At the age of thirteen, Jack Kennedy was writing home from boarding school —and he knew exactly what his father wanted to hear. Top marks *and* top athletic performance, both were expected of him. So if he bragged a little about the game he had just played, he thought, that was all right.

Another boy in young John Fitzgerald Kennedy's place might have not even gone out for football. Jack just didn't have the weight to make the first team; he was tall enough, but no amount of ice cream seemed to add pounds to his skinny frame.

Nevertheless, Jack turned up doggedly for afternoon practice. By pure will power, he managed to give heavier fellows a hard time on the field. Because he had always had a certain problem, he was used to facing extra odds.

The problem was his brother Joe.

Joe was two years older than Jack, and he was stronger and heavier. He got better marks too. Whatever Joe tried, he seemed almost effortlessly to shine at; he was outstanding in every way. Sometimes Jack had the idea that ever since

the day he was born, on May 29, 1917, he had been trying to beat Joe at something.

Why not just give up then? Jack did from time to time decide he might as well. When it came to school, he did sometimes take the easier way. "He is casual and disorderly," his housemaster reported one term. "Jack studies at the last minute, keeps appointments late, has little sense of material values, and can seldom locate his possessions."

Despite such harsh comments, though, his parents refused to be discouraged about their second son.

"Now, Jack," Mr. Kennedy wrote, "I don't want to give the impression that I am a nagger, for goodness knows I think that is the worst thing any parent can be." Then he added: "After long experience in sizing up people I definitely know you have the goods and you can go a long way. Now aren't you foolish not to get all there is out of what God has given you . . ."

The tone his father took had a great effect on Jack. As was the case with all nine of his children, Mr. Kennedy exerted a constant influence—and he was a powerful man.

His own father had stepped off a boat

Even in grade school Jack played hard for his team, as shown by the knees of his uniform.

from Ireland in 1848, penniless but determined to make a name for himself. That he did in Boston politics, and he also made enough money in the whiskey business to send his son to Harvard. The son, in turn, set his own mind on other goals.

Joseph P. Kennedy—Jack's father— had as his first aim becoming a millionaire. By shrewd dealing in the stock market, he accomplished this by the time he was thirty, and then he kept right on working until his fortune was among the world's largest. Yet mere wealth could not satisfy him.

His further goal was political. But the limited scope afforded by Boston politics could not content him any more than being only comfortably well-off could. Although religion was not supposed to have any bearing on a candidate's chances in the United States, no Roman Catholic had ever been elected President, and the Kennedys were faithful Catholics. Still Mr. Kennedy wanted nothing less than the Presidency—if not for himself, then for a son of his.

Joe Jr., his oldest and by even impartial verdict an exceptional lad, bore the brunt of Mr. Kennedy's prodding. Nevertheless, the father had ambition galore; he drove all of his children to excel.

"When the going gets tough," he told them, "the tough get going."

But for all his fierce ambition, Mr. Kennedy loved his children devotedly and showed each of them how much he valued them. He would leave almost any business conference to attend and applaud if one of them took part in a school play. And even if the best Jack could do in football was the junior varsity, his father cheered him on with enormous enthusiasm.

It was while working out with the JVs at Harvard that Jack injured his back.

He hit the ground hard during a scrimmage. Although he refused to admit he was hurt, forcing himself to smile as he slowly stood up unaided, he never got over the effects of that fall.

Three years later, he tried to enlist in the Army or Navy; but he was turned down because doctors thought his back could not take the strain of active duty. Jack Kennedy thought otherwise. It was the summer of 1941, and the terrible war that had torn Europe for almost two years threatened to involve America. From the vantage point of London, where his father had been serving as United States Ambassador, Jack had seen some of the horror firsthand. He

4

A picture of high spirits, Jack (left) and Joe Jr. prepare to cross the Atlantic with their father, then U.S. Ambassador to Great Britain.

had even written a book, *Why England Slept,* which had—surprisingly, considering he was only twenty-three—become a best seller.

With the book's success, for the first time Jack no longer felt overshadowed by his brother Joe. But the increasing threat of war made writing seem less important. Joe, of course, had had no trouble in getting accepted by the Naval Air Corps and was already training to be a pilot. Just as doggedly as he had gone out for football a few years earlier, Jack Kennedy began working on his own now to convince the Navy to take him.

For five months, he grimly exercised every day. Then he passed the Navy's physical-fitness test, only to find himself shunted into a desk job.

After Pearl Harbor put the United States actively in the war, Lieutenant Kennedy refused to keep on writing reports, and for once he badgered his father. Get me on a ship, he begged. Picking up a telephone, Mr. Kennedy called one of his influential friends. Within a few months, Lieutenant Jack Kennedy was enrolled at the Motor Torpedo Boat Squadron Training Center at Melville, Rhode Island. A few months later he left San Francisco, bound for the South Pacific.

In the palm-fringed harbor of the tropical island of Tulagi, the young lieutenant took command of PT 109.

Small and grimy, already scarred from dozens of patrol missions in the Guadalcanal area, the boat still had a glamor

5

about it because of the daredevil reputation that patrol torpedo craft had earned in Philippine waters. So swift and maneuverable that they could sneak up and torpedo larger vessels, the PTs had seized the imagination of the American public early in the war, when American successes were pitifully few. Vacationing on Cape Cod, Jack Kennedy had seen one on exhibit and he, too, had been impressed. But the Navy had a better reason than merely gratifying the whim of a rich young lieutenant when it made him skipper of his own PT boat.

Summer after summer at Cape Cod, Jack Kennedy had sailed in every kind of weather. Silver cups for first prize in sailing races were highly valued in the Kennedy household, and Jack had taken more than his share. He was an expert sailor, so even if he looked much too boyish to be an officer, let alone a skipper, his crew soon understood that he deserved the assignment. Skinny as he still was, he showed the steady nerves of a stalwart veteran when he took PT 109

A PT boat

out on nightly patrols. The Japanese were desperately trying to bring in supplies to their Solomon Islands bases, and the mission of the PTs was to harass the enemy shipping.

Night after night, Kennedy would slip past shadowy black islands, peering to see a sign of enemy supply barges. In the darkness, shapes suddenly loomed up. Were they real or imaginary? Were they friend or foe? After he ordered his gunners to fire on an enemy target, it was often too dangerous to wait to see if the target was hit. Sometimes PT 109 was fired upon as Lieutenant Kennedy veered off, and there was never an instant out on the inky sea when he could relax.

Then in the early morning of August 2, 1943, the slender mast of a Japanese destroyer loomed dead ahead.

"Sound general quarters," Kennedy ordered. That meant: be ready to fight.

But there was no time to maneuver or fight back. Within seconds, the *Amagiri* rammed the smaller vessel. The impact loosed Kennedy's hands from the wheel and hurled him against a steel plate. His back was hurt again, but he had no time to think of himself.

"Everybody into the water!" he shouted.

He dove and tried to avoid the eerie patches of burning oil as he swam about, rounding up the ten other men who had survived the crash. Two in the crew never were found. Among the survivors, several had been seriously hurt. One of them, a wiry gunner's mate from Boston, gasped to the skipper:

"I can't go any further."

"For a guy from Boston, you're certainly putting up a great exhibition out here, Harris," Kennedy purposely taunted him. Gripping his arm, Kennedy then pulled off the sailor's heavy shoes and jacket and towed him along.

Part of PT 109, inclined at a sharp angle, remained above water; and during darkness Kennedy assembled the remnants of his crew on the slanting deck. But with the coming of light, he knew they were too exposed for safety. On several of the tiny islands in the area, there would be Japanese who might spot them.

"Back into the water," he said. Hanging on to the hull with their fingers, the eleven talked over their chances. The Japanese were a deadly menace, but so were sharks. The hull kept listing more sharply; it was bound to sink before nightfall. By about noon, Kennedy decided they would have to swim for it.

Knowing the waters as well as he did, he suggested a dot of land known as Plum Pudding Island for their goal. But how could Harris and the other wounded make it? The worst case was Pat McMahon, at thirty-seven the oldest in the crew and thus "Pop" to the rest. Pop was an expert mechanic who in his best days was not much of a swimmer; with the severe burns he had suffered, he could hardly move on his own. While others helped Harris, Lieutenant Kennedy rigged up a strap harness around Pop and took the end of the strap in his own teeth.

And for the next four hours he swam the breast stroke, tugging Pop along in the water beside him, three and a half miles to the little island. Near sundown, all eleven reached the beach.

"I'm okay, Mr. Kennedy," Pop gasped. "How about you?"

During the ensuing week, Jack Kennedy showed the answer. Never once mentioning his own aching back, he swam out into the channel again that very night, alone, in a vain effort to find a friendly PT patrol boat. When this attempt failed, he led his men to another nearby island where he hoped it might be easier to attract rescuers. With no food except coconut milk, with McMahon's burns festering dangerously, their plight was awful. Japanese scouts might find them at any moment, and the tiny party of Americans had no weapons to fight with. But Lieutenant Kennedy never stopped trying to keep up his men's hopes.

After four days of constant but vain effort to find help, fate sent him the means. Sighting two natives in a canoe, Kennedy took the chance that they might be friendly. He grabbed a coconut husk and carved on it with his sheath knife:

NAURO ISL
NATIVE KNOWS POSIT
HE CAN PILOT   11 ALIVE NEED
SMALL BOAT

KENNEDY

Three days later the gaunt, feverish, exhausted crew of PT 109 arrived back at their base.

Following the rescue, Kennedy soon returned to active patrol duty on another PT; but within a few months, even he had to admit his back needed attention. Soon he was a patient in a Navy hospital in Massachusetts, able to visit his family in their Cape Cod house on weekends.

Exactly one year after PT 109 went down, two priests came on a somber mission to the Kennedy home.

In the sky over the English Channel, another Lieutenant Kennedy had lost his life. Joe Jr., on whom so many high hopes had been centered, would never return from the war.

Jack Kennedy had been thinking of becoming a newspaper writer or perhaps a college professor after his release from the Navy. One or the other would suit him, he thought, and neither would put undue strain on his weak back, which he now knew would always pain him. But the death of his brother changed everything.

Despite the rivalry between them in boyhood, Joe and Jack had become more than good friends. The loss Jack now felt was so deep that he spent many months gathering tributes from those who had known Joe well, and he tried to ease his own sorrow by putting these words into a small book, *As We Remember Joe*.

In later years, some said it was Jack's father who made the decision during these months that his oldest surviving son must go into politics; others said Jack Kennedy made the decision all on his own, because he wanted to carry on in Joe's place. But most outsiders were not aware of one fact that had to influence both father and son. This was the hard medical fact that Jack's back just might not be able to take the rigors of active campaigning.

No matter what his father's advice, only Jack Kennedy himself could have willed himself to go ahead, regardless of how much his back hurt. In his first political campaign, when he ran at the age of twenty-eight for a seat in the House of Representatives, the young candidate smiled and shook hands for fourteen hours at a stretch—and hardly anybody suspected that the main thought in his mind was of the steaming hot bath at midnight which would ease his constant backache.

Winning his race for election was comparatively easy, otherwise. For Jack was running in the Boston district where both his grandfathers had been big men. His mother's father, former mayor "Honey Fitz" Fitzgerald, was still around to slap voters on the back and urge them to elect his grandson.

But the rest of the family did even more to win friends for their candidate. In a tireless marathon, Jack's brothers and sisters spoke up for him at street-corner meetings. His mother invited hundreds of women to tea and talked politics with them. His father was on the telephone day and night, mustering votes for Jack. Having attracted much unfriendly publicity by feuding publicly with President Franklin Roosevelt, Mr. Kennedy stayed in the background, but his telephone connections and his checkbook were constantly in use for his son's cause.

Three times Jack Kennedy won easily as Congressman from East Boston. Then in 1952 he took his first big political gamble. He decided to run for the Senate, even though he would face a formidable Republican opponent—Henry Cabot Lodge, the bearer of two old and honored Massachusetts names. But with all of the Kennedy resources mobilized to campaign throughout the state, Jack did not have too much trouble in defeating Lodge. At the age of thirty-five, the former PT skipper took his seat in the United States Senate.

It was as Senator Kennedy that he first attracted national attention. Still so young-looking that he was sometimes mistaken for a page boy, he was also handsome enough to cause magazines to call him "the Senate's most eligible bachelor." When he ended that by marrying a beautiful society girl named Jacqueline Bouvier, the wedding drew such crowds of the curious that it made front-page news. Not long afterward, he made news of another sort.

Gradually his back had weakened to the extent that he could no longer walk without crutches. Outwardly the picture of vigorous young manhood, he hated the thought of being an invalid. When doctors told him a spinal operation might possibly help, but that the surgery would be extremely dangerous, he did not hesitate. Slapping his crutches with his fist, he said: "I'd rather die than spend the rest of my life on these things."

And he nearly died in 1954. Twice after the operation, his wife and parents were told he had no chance. Twice a priest was summoned to give him the last rites of his church. But Jack Kennedy recovered both times.

During the long months of painful convalescence, as he lay flat on his back, he mused about many things to keep his mind off his own troubles. From these reflections came a book describing several episodes in American history, when various Senators defied popular opinion to stand up for a cause they believed was

Mrs. John Kennedy holds her husband's X-rays as he enters the hospital for an operation on his back.

right. *Profiles in Courage* the book was called, and it won John F. Kennedy a Pulitzer Prize. It also caused the widespread circulation of a cutting remark—that the young Senator would do well if he himself showed "less profile and more courage."

For up until this time, he had not impressed many voters as a particularly able battler for any cause. On the burning issue of McCarthyism—the ruthless hounding of alleged Communists by

9

John F. Kennedy is sworn in as 35th President of the United States.

Senator Joseph R. McCarthy of Wisconsin—Senator Kennedy had kept utterly silent. His father was a friend of McCarthy, and many scoffed that Jack Kennedy was still completely under his father's thumb. Other voters, inspired by varying degrees of prejudice, opposed Kennedy because he was a Catholic.

That he had been a war hero was granted. But it took John F. Kennedy much longer to prove that as a political figure he was also courageous.

He wanted no credit for his private battle with his bad back; only those closest to him ever knew his back still pained him steadily, although the operation had made it possible for him to walk again without crutches.

What Jack Kennedy did want, from the time he recovered after almost dying, was to become President.

And ambitiously, efficiently, but above all, excitingly, he proceeded to convince the American public that he deserved

10

the chance. He did so by offering sign after sign that he had matured politically. He spoke up often in favor of forward-looking programs. He met the issue of his Catholicism head-on, openly proclaiming his independence from any possible clerical dictation. With good humor, but decisively, he let everybody know he honored his father—yet took no important political advice from him.

It was as the vigorous spokesman for the new generation in America that he campaigned for the Presidency.

He was so handsome and quick to smile, he had so lively a wit and so beautiful a wife, he defied staid tradition so easily that "the Kennedy style" became a watchword on the political scene.

By a thin margin, yet with a rare sense of excitement, the American people chose John F. Kennedy as their President in November of 1960. Then during the brief time he was given in the White House, he brought the United States and the world a new vision—he opened a "new frontier," in his own phrase.

Three years plus two weeks after his election, his life ended. But the memory of Jack Kennedy still inspires many millions of people everywhere.

CHARLES A. LINDBERGH
Lone Eagle of the Atlantic

A small gray airplane started slowly down the runway. Mechanics ran along beside it, pushing at the wings. They were actually trying to help the engine gain speed. That was clear to every person in the crowd watching tensely from the edge of the field.

They all knew the little plane was overloaded, not with passengers or cargo —but with gas. It had been specially built with an extra-large fuel tank, which had just been filled to capacity for the first time. Would the extra weight prevent a takeoff? Nobody could be sure.

In the cockpit, Charles Augustus Lindbergh Jr. pulled back on his control stick as the plane picked up speed. The wheels left the ground, but then they touched again. He was almost at the end of the runway; he would crash if not airborne within a few seconds. Then gradually, ever so gradually, the plane lifted, clearing the telephone wires at the end of the field by only twenty feet before soaring higher over the trees on the hilltop beyond.

Lindbergh was on his way! It was May 20, 1927, and he was starting on a solo flight from New York to Paris.

Already six men had died in attempts to fly the same course nonstop. About 3600 miles had to be covered, and at the rate of speed the best planes of the day could muster, the flight had to take at least thirty hours. For a pilot daring enough to attempt the feat by himself, fatigue was even more of a menace than weather conditions; it would be impossible to relax for even a few minutes during a long night, the next day and the following evening.

Flying the Atlantic Ocean was not in itself the challenge. Already sixty-six men, including the crews of two dirigibles, had done it; but no man had flown the ocean alone. Two Englishmen had flown the 1900 miles from Newfoundland to Ireland; but this tall, lanky young pilot from Minnesota intended to fly the much longer distance from New York to Paris—almost twice as far.

Too busy for the first few minutes to reflect on the dangerous hours ahead, Lindbergh checked his instrument panel carefully. Oil pressure, fifty-six pounds . . . oil temperature, thirty-four degrees . . . tachometer, 1750 revolutions per minute . . . altitude, 200 feet. All normal, so far.

Looking out then, he was astonished to see a plane flying right beside him, taking pictures. It had been chartered by a newspaper—for, on this day, Charles Lindbergh was headline material. People everywhere were waiting anxiously to find out if he could make good on his gamble.

Within a few minutes, Lindbergh left the newspaper plane behind; in a sense he left the world behind. He was alone with his plane, alone in the sky. That suited him. Ever since boyhood, he had liked being on his own and he had agreed with his father's advice against depending too heavily on others. He remembered, too, the old Minnesota saying: "One boy's a boy; two boys are half a boy; three boys are no boy at all."

Although Minnesota was the state he called home, Lindbergh had been born in Detroit, Michigan, on February 4, 1902. His father was Charles Augustus Lindbergh, who later became a crusading member of the House of Representatives. His mother was a schoolteacher. As a boy Lindbergh was shy, given to rambling in the woods alone. Later he spent two years at the University of Wisconsin studying engineering, before enrolling as an air cadet in the Army in 1924.

First in the Army, then as a civilian pilot, he dared the unknown almost every day. With the air age still so young, the perils of flying mail planes at this period were as great as those faced by the Pony Express riders of earlier times. But Lindberg craved the challenge of testing himself; he could not be content even with mail runs. It was during an otherwise uneventful flight between St. Louis and Chicago that he thought of trying the Atlantic crossing.

He knew he could do it if—if he could find men of means to back him. He would need a special sort of plane for such a venture, and he had no money of his own to buy one. But investing in him would be a good risk, of that he was positive. Ever since 1919, a prize of $25,000 had been on offer for the first nonstop flight between New York and Paris. Lindbergh had not the slightest doubt that he could win the prize.

After several months, he did manage to convince friends and bankers in St. Louis to help him. Then he spent several more months supervising the construction of a new plane. It was a single-engine craft, powered by a Wright Whirlwind engine, built to his order by Ryan Airlines of California. When it was finished, he named it the *Spirit of St. Louis.*

By the time Lindbergh flew his new plane into New York, it was the spring of 1927. Several other men, better known by far than he was, were also preparing for a transatlantic flight. Commander Richard E. Byrd was almost ready with his trimotored Fokker, the *America.* Clarence Chamberlain, who had just set a new air endurance record with his *Columbia,* was tuning it up for the big flight. Lindbergh's plane was the smallest. It had a single engine; it had no radio, nor any sextant for navigation.

But Lindbergh, the man least likely to succeed, stirred the imagination of the press, the public and the aviation world. He was only twenty-five, unassuming and handsome, with hair never quite combed and a shy, boyish smile. They called him all sorts of nicknames—"Lucky Lindy" and "The Flying Kid" and "The Lone Eagle." Beneath his boyish appearance,

14

Final preparations included fueling the Spirit of St. Louis *before Lindbergh's transatlantic flight.*

however, was a careful, methodical man. While his competitors squabbled and fussed with more tests, Lindbergh calmly went ahead with his own preparations. As soon as the weather cleared, he took off.

As the news of his departure flashed around the world, people in many countries paused in whatever they were doing to discuss his chances for success. They gathered in front of newspaper offices to get the latest word; thousands kept their radios tuned in for the latest bulletin. In Paris a newspaper commented that Lindbergh's calm courage recalled to French minds the brave Americans they had known as doughboys during World War I.

Aloft in his *Spirit of St. Louis,* the object of all this attention flew steadily onward. He passed over New England, Nova Scotia and Newfoundland, and his legs grew stiff and cramped. Hour after hour, he got sleepier. But he shook his head, stamped his feet, flexed his muscles, stayed awake. Twelve hours out, he flew over the last tip of land he could expect to spy until Ireland. As he veered eastward over the vast Atlantic, one-third of his flight was completed; but by far the most dangerous part lay ahead.

Climbing above a low fog, he flew onward in the dark night, wondering if man ever escaped his worldly bonds as completely as when flying alone through the darkness. He mused about his parents, about his own early flying days; he almost forgot where he was. Then suddenly he noticed it was getting cold. And he saw ice forming on his wings.

15

Ice was his worst enemy, he knew. Ice caked on his wings could make the plane too heavy to fly, too heavy to control. Slowly and cautiously, Lindbergh came down lower, where the ice danger would be less.

At 1:52 A.M. he noted in his log: "Eighteen hundred miles behind. Eighteen hundred miles to go." He was halfway to Paris. He had a bag of five sandwiches with him, but he did not feel hungry. He was not even thirsty. The only thought his mind could hold was that he had to stay awake and keep flying.

With the sunrise, the problem of fighting off sleep became even more urgent. He flexed his arms and legs, bounced up and down in his seat, finally pushed his head out of the window to get more air. It was a matter of life itself to remain awake.

At times he thought he saw land below, but he knew it must be a mirage. Finally, twenty-seven hours out of New York, he spotted some sea gulls in the distance—a sure sign of land ahead. Then black specks on the water, fishing boats. He dived to only fifty feet above the billowing Atlantic and circled, idling his engine. Three times he flew over the tiny boats, leaning out of his window. He even yelled: "Which way is Ireland?" But nobody came above deck, nobody answered him.

An hour later, he clearly saw a strip of purplish blue in the haze ahead. He had turned out over the ocean off Newfoundland sixteen hours earlier, and was allowing eighteen hours to reach Ireland. If this really was land, he was two hours ahead of schedule.

It was land. Lindbergh had safely crossed the ocean.

Checking his chart, he saw he had arrived over the southwest coast of Ireland, only three miles off course, almost a perfect landfall. Wide awake now, he angled his plane for the English Channel—and France.

In Paris word spread that the little plane had been spotted over Ireland. Lindbergh was on his way! Thousands upon thousands of Frenchmen suddenly had the same thought and started for Le Bourget airfield outside Paris, where he would land. Two companies of soldiers had to be ordered out to control the crowds.

As dusk fell, Lindbergh flew over the English Channel. For the first time, he began thinking of what he would do in Paris: first he would put his plane in a hangar, then send a cable home, then try to find a place to sleep. He had not the slightest idea that the entire world was following his flight minute by minute, that an enormous mob was already waiting to welcome him.

Flying at an altitude of 4,000 feet, Lindbergh spotted the Eiffel Tower even before he had expected to and began circling to come down. His landing wheels touched at Le Bourget at 10:24 P.M., thirty-three hours and thirty minutes after his departure from New York.

As the plane stopped, Lindbergh was astounded to see the entire field covered with people. Only the runway had been kept clear, and now crowds were swarming right up to his plane. Completely baffled, he opened his cockpit window.

"Are there any mechanics here?" he asked.

The only reply was a roar of voices.

16

The Spirit of St. Louis *over Belgium*.

"Does anyone here speak English?" Lindbergh shouted.

Cheers and noise again drowned out his words. Confused even more, Lindbergh began climbing out of his plane. He suddenly found himself lying on his back above the crowd, held aloft by unknown hands. It was an utterly strange sensation. At first, he feared he might be dropped, but there seemed no sense in struggling. Relaxing, he let himself be carried along above a sea of fully 100,000 Frenchmen; finally he was put down, and two French aviators conducted him into an airport office. There the American Ambassador to France greeted him.

Meanwhile, back in the United States every newspaper was rushing special editions onto the streets. Using its biggest headline type, *The New York Times* proclaimed: "LINDBERGH DOES IT! TO PARIS IN 33½ HOURS; FLIES 1,000 MILES THROUGH SNOW AND SLEET; CHEERING FRENCH CARRY HIM OFF FIELD."

To his own amazement, but nobody else's, Lindbergh had become one of the great heroes of his time. Millions of his own countrymen and millions more throughout the world took him to their hearts, as one commentator said, "as they had no other human being in living memory."

President Calvin Coolidge sent the U.S.S. *Memphis* to bring him home. As the ship steamed into Chesapeake Bay on June 11, Lindbergh said to a reporter: "It's good to go back to being just Charlie Lindbergh again."

The reporter smiled. "I'm afraid," he

17

Anne Morrow Lindbergh joined her husband on many flights.

said, "you can never go back completely now."

The reporter was right. Homecoming for Lindbergh was a fantastic experience. In New York City a ticker-tape parade dwarfed all previous receptions for distinguished visitors. Practically every honor that anyone could think of was heaped on Lindbergh. He received the Medal of Honor of the Congress of the United States and 116 other medals; he was promoted to colonel in the Air Force Reserve; he was mentioned for every political office, including that of President.

Still boyish-looking and unassuming

despite all of the acclaim, Lindbergh made several goodwill tours in the months that followed. Among the tours was one to Mexico, where he met Anne Morrow, the daughter of the United States Ambassador. Later they were married. He became an adviser to many aviation companies and tried to settle down to a quiet life, but this proved impossible.

With his wife and baby son, who had been born on June 22, 1930, Lindbergh was living outside of Hopewell, New Jersey, when a spectacular crime put him back on newspaper front pages. A kidnapper had stolen into his home, had taken his 2-year-old son and was demanding $50,000 in ransom.

One of the largest manhunts in the nation's history immediately started, and it ended two months later with the discovery of the dead child. His body was found in a patch of woods about five miles from the Lindbergh home.

Further adding to the parents' anguish, they had to relive the horror two years later when the kidnapper, Bruno Richard Hauptman, was captured, tried, convicted and executed.

The crushing nature of the publicity to which the Lindberghs had been submitted caused them to leave the United States in 1936 to make a new home in England. There they found it easier to live in privacy with their other children.

In the years that followed, it became increasingly clear that Germany was rearming and taking the path toward war. During this period, a secret request went out to Lindbergh from United States intelligence officials. Would he go to Germany to find out what he could about the German air force? Although living in England, Lindbergh was still a colonel in the United States Air Force Reserve; he consented to make the trip.

Before the eyes of the world once more, Lindbergh was received in Germany by Marshal Hermann Goering, chief of the German air force, who proudly displayed his country's expanding air might. The Nazis also gave Lindbergh the Order of the German Eagle, and his acceptance of the medal stirred criticism in the United States among those already certain that Germany was democracy's enemy. It could not be divulged at the time that Lindbergh was on a secret and official mission, which might not succeed if he offended his German hosts.

When war did break out in Europe, Lindbergh further antagonized the same critics in the United States. Having been genuinely impressed by German's military power, the aviation hero joined a group known as the America First Committee, which had been formed to try to keep the United States from giving any sort of support to England and France. Although the United States maintained its policy of neutrality during the early months of World War II, sentiment throughout the country generally favored the Allied cause. When Lindbergh continued to speak for the America First Committee, President Franklin D. Roosevelt called him "a copperhead" —a term used during the Civil War to describe Northerners who took the Southern side.

Then Lindbergh wrote to the President, saying that under the circumstances he felt he should resign his Reserve commission. The resignation was accepted.

After Pearl Harbor, when the United States entered the war, Lindbergh tried to get back into service. His application never was accepted. Instead he went to work as a civilian technician for an aviation company, a job which took him into the Pacific combat area. As a civilian he managed to fly several combat missions against the Japanese; on one of these, he shot down a Japanese plane. He was then forty-two years old.

After the war Lindbergh tried once more to settle down to private life in the United States. He and his family moved to Connecticut, where they had a house in a secluded suburb. In 1954 President Dwight D. Eisenhower commissioned him a brigadier general in the Air Force Reserve. Lindbergh was then working as a consultant for airplane companies.

In the same year, Lindbergh wrote a book about his transatlantic flight, *The Spirit of St. Louis*, which won the Pulitzer Prize for biography. Other than that, he shunned publicity and interviews to such an extent that today many young people know nothing of him beyond his name.

Yet any visitor to the Smithsonian Institution in Washington can see his plane. Hanging from the ceiling of the government museum is the original *Spirit of St. Louis*, a tiny craft compared with today's giants. Almost all who see it marvel at its small size and at the daring of the man who flew it across the Atlantic. To them and others with long memories, Charles A. Lindbergh is the embodiment of the American ideal of modesty, courage and accomplishment.

MARTIN LUTHER KING
"I Have a Dream"

On Thursday evening, December 1, 1955, a crowded bus stopped at a downtown corner in Montgomery, Alabama. Some white persons stepped aboard, paid their fares and looked for empty seats; there were none. So the driver ordered several Negroes sitting near the front to stand, in order that white passengers could take their seats. That was the way things always had been in Montgomery and other cities of the South.

Three of the Negroes on the bus got up as usual, but one woman refused. She was Mrs. Rosa Parks, a seamstress. She had been bending over a sewing machine all day and her back hurt.

"Why should I have to stand?" Mrs. Parks asked. "Why should we be pushed around?"

"The law's the law," said the bus driver.

He asked her again to stand, and again she refused. Then he called the police, who arrested Mrs. Parks. She had violated a state law requiring passengers to follow the directions of a bus driver. In due course she was taken to the city jail, and fingerprinted and photographed before being released on bail later the same evening.

Mrs. Rosa Parks had no notion that she was opening a new chapter in American history. She had spoken up on the spur of the moment, simply because she was tired. Yet her protest touched off one of the great human dramas of modern times—the struggle by the Negroes of the United States to win their own freedom. It also catapulted a young Negro minister to international fame.

The Reverend Martin Luther King Jr. was twenty-seven years old in 1955. He had only recently finished his religious training and come to Montgomery as pastor of the Dexter Avenue Baptist Church. But if ever there was a case of the right man appearing at the right time in the right place, this was it.

It might have seemed at first glance that the new young preacher would never make much of a leader. He was short and stocky, with no air of command. His voice seemed too soft, his manner too gentle, to attract attention. He had had little experience in addressing audiences.

Perhaps there were some who sensed immediately that this quiet man had hidden strength. Or, as the more politically minded put it, probably his main appeal was merely that he had not been in town long enough to make any enemies. Whatever the reason, he was chosen soon after Mrs. Parks was arrested to be chairman of a mass protest.

That in itself was unusual. Negroes were not supposed to hold meetings or plan protests. According to the majority of white Southerners, Negroes were not discontented with their place in Southern society; to keep the peace, most Negroes did not openly dispute the point. But by December 1955, change was in the wind.

Almost a century after the Civil War, the Negroes of the United States were still treated as second-class citizens, deprived of equal opportunities in many areas of national life. But the Supreme Court had recently decreed that all children, black as well as white, were entitled to the same schooling. A new generation of Negro college students was

Led by Dr. King, Negro parents escort children to newly integrated schools.

restlessly debating how best to press for decent jobs and housing. Even many of their parents were getting impatient with politicians who told them improvements must come gradually.

Thus the arrest of Mrs. Parks struck sparks that might earlier have failed to ignite. As word of what had happened sped through the Negro community of Montgomery on that cold December evening, heated questions kept being asked: "Can't we do something?" "What *can* we do?"

To young Dr. King, the charged atmosphere presented an awesome opportunity. In his college library, he had come under the spell of one of the great leaders of the modern era, Mahatma Gandhi of India. Like Jesus of Nazareth, Gandhi preached love rather than hate, peaceful protest rather than violence. These two men must be the inspiration for the Negroes of America, Dr. King passionately believed. So when he was asked to direct the mass protest, he saw his selection as providing just the chance he had dreamed of to bring Gandhi's message to his own people.

But what could the Negroes of Montgomery do along the lines of peaceful protest to show the resentment they all felt about the way they were treated?

Since the question had been raised in the first place over bus seats, the answer concentrated on the same issue. At a series of emergency meetings in Dr. King's Dexter Avenue church, it was agreed that Negroes would not pay a penny in bus fares—until every seat on every bus was put on a first-come-first-served basis.

The first meeting was held on a Friday

evening, and on Monday morning the bus boycott began. To get Negro wage-earners to their jobs, car pools had to be set up; horses, even mule carts were pressed into service to make up for the shortage of Negro-owned automobiles. Pickup stations around the city had to be established. To a surprising extent, the makeshift transportation arrangements accomplished their mission on Monday. Negroes who could not manage to get rides still refused to board a bus; instead, they walked.

The spectacle of Negroes uniting this way astonished white Montgomery. Everybody knew that Negroes were not capable of organizing anything on their own, numerous white Southerners assured one another. Then, as day after day the boycott continued in full force, ridicule gave way to fear and bullying. Negro car-pool drivers were threatened, even by the police. Dr. King himself was arrested on a charge of speeding.

Faced by the hardening opposition of the white community, Martin Luther King Jr. had to pass his first big test as a leader.

As a boy in Atlanta, Georgia, where he had been born on January 15, 1929, he had wanted to be a fireman. But he was the son of a minister, who trained him to think of his responsibility to help other Negroes. For a time the boy considered becoming a doctor, then a lawyer. But while he was at college he turned to religion as the best means for being of service.

At the Crozer Theological Seminary in Pennsylvania, he felt increasingly sure that Christian love could bring brotherhood on earth. One of six Negroes among a hundred whites in the school, he worked at his books day and night to prove himself; and on graduating he was first in his class as well as president of the student body. To prepare himself still further, he studied at Boston University for a doctor's degree before moving to Montgomery.

Dr. King had comparatively little leading to do in the first days of the boycott. The entire Negro community was so fired with enthusiasm that people willingly got up earlier than usual, and willingly trudged many miles to and from work if necessary. The main need was for efficient managing of car-pool schedules and other such details—managing which Dr. King cheerfully admitted was not his strong point.

But with each succeeding week, as the Negroes refused to give in and white anger kept rising, ugly incidents became increasingly common. White rowdies taunted Negro drivers constantly, and the danger of violence grew more menacing. Then Dr. King's courage under stress attracted notice far beyond the borders of Alabama.

The climax came one night in February, when a dynamite bomb exploded on Dr. King's own front porch, showering broken glass and bricks in every direction. Had he been at home, he might have been seriously injured. Until that night the Negroes of Montgomery had heeded Dr. King's words cautioning against any outbursts of violence, but after the blast a crowd of Negroes massed in front of the house. Their mood seemed to have changed with the threat to their leader, and the police on the scene tried in vain to disperse them. It looked as if rioting was bound to start.

A white bystander ran off and searched out Dr. King, who had been attending a meeting elsewhere. A few minutes later, Dr. King stood on his shattered front porch and spoke to his followers:

"Please be peaceful," he pleaded. "I want you to love our enemies. Be good to them. Love them and let them know you love them."

He paused, then continued:

"I did not start this boycott. I was asked by you to serve as your spokesman. I want it to be known the length and breadth of the land that if I am stopped, this movement will not stop. If I am stopped, our work will not stop, for what we are doing is right. What we are doing is just—and God is with us."

Having heard these words, the crowd that had been unruly walked slowly and peacefully homeward. The police relaxed. And throughout the United States, many thousands read the words in their newspapers, or heard them repeated on television. Overnight the nation learned that Martin Luther King Jr., the man who spoke of nonviolence, believed in it even when his own life was endangered. In the North especially, many whose skins were not dark were stirred by the courage of Dr. King and his supporters.

"Nonviolence is our testing point," Dr. King said repeatedly. "The strong man is the man who can stand up for his rights and not hit back."

In an era facing problems undreamed of by previous generations, Dr. King more and more seemed to be demon-strating heroism of a new order.

As for the bus boycott that had brought him national attention and acclaim, it went on and on despite several lawsuits brought by the bus company. Rosa Parks, who had started it all, was fined $14 for refusing to obey a bus driver, but still the mass boycott continued. Finally, in November 1956, nearly a year after Mrs. Parks had refused to give up her seat, the United States Supreme Court declared that bus segregation in Montgomery and elsewhere was illegal.

Negroes began to ride the buses once more, sitting where they pleased. Dr. King's faith in nonviolence had been triumphantly vindicated.

For America's Negroes, Dr. King himself now became the voice of hope, promising that a whole long list of injustices could be overcome by nonviolent resistance.

For many whites, Dr. King was the voice of conscience. He made them see the conflict between their religious and political beliefs in the equality of man—and the plain facts of prejudice and discrimination.

As the leading symbol of the fight for racial equality, Dr. King also became a target for abuse and attack. On his travels to and from speaking engagements, he was spat upon and jeered at; he was even struck and kicked. Once he was stabbed, almost fatally, by a deranged Negro woman. Frequently he was jailed for short periods. Threats became so common that his wife Coretta learned to ignore foul-mouthed telephone calls, and even a Ku Klux Klan cross burning on their front lawn.

In front of his house, Dr. King pulls up a four-foot cross burned by Ku Klux Klan members. His two-year-old son watches.

Despite all this, Dr. King never wavered in his faith that passive resistance would conquer violence. He traveled around the world to spread his message, based on the Bible and the teachings of Gandhi. He wrote books; he spoke everywhere.

He had his critics, of course. They said he was poor at running an efficient office, a criticism he willingly admitted. Others in the civil-rights movement suggested that many other Negroes were also working hard to fight segregation, without the acclaim that was showered on Dr. King. And some Negro extremists called his passive-resistance movement a form of servility to white oppressors, an argument that found little acceptance elsewhere.

Ceaselessly busy, Dr. King wrote a book, *Stride Toward Freedom,* about his experiences in Montgomery. He organized the Southern Christian Leadership Conference, which helped to found the Student Nonviolent Coordinating Committee; these spearheaded increasingly active drives for Negro voter registration throughout the South. But Dr. King's boldest campaign took place in Birmingham, Alabama. Many observers thought Birmingham was the worst city in the South, as far as its treatment of Negroes was concerned.

On April 1, 1963, under Dr. King's leadership, Birmingham Negroes began constant picketing and protest marches in order to call attention to their grievances about limited job opportunities and segregation in schools, stores, restaurants and theaters. Day after day, Negro men, women and children—some children as young as seven—paraded

downtown, chanting: "March, march, march for freedom." Day after day the marchers were jailed for violating city laws. They went off to jail singing, while Dr. King tried to reason with civic leaders behind the scenes. Even the young children seemed inspired by Dr. King's pledge that he would keep leading the demonstrations until "Pharaoh lets God's children go."

Then on a sunny day in May, about 2,500 Negroes gathered in Kelly Ingam Park in the Negro district of Birmingham. Mostly children and students, they took to shouting taunts at policemen detailed to watch them. The police were under the command of T. Eugene Connor; a burly fellow, he was known by all Birmingham as "Bull" Connor.

Connor and his police were prepared for trouble on that sunny afternoon.

They held five German shepherd dogs, straining on leashes. An armored car that looked like a tank rumbled nearby. Firemen had been summoned, and they held high-pressure hoses capable of spraying fierce jets of water.

"Freedom!" The shout came from a Negro boy.

At that instant, a few Negroes began to throw rocks at the policemen.

"Let 'em have it!" The order came from Bull Connor.

A powerful stream of water ripped into the crowd. The pressure was so great that water skinned the bark off many trees in the park. Negroes tumbled to the ground, some of them injured. Many others started running wildly. They were pushed back, but some threw rocks or bottles at the police. The police dogs barked furiously, although they were still held on leash.

But newspapers in every part of the world reported the next day that dogs and hoses had been used on the assembled Negroes, most of them children. So Dr. King had succeeded in focusing wide attention on Birmingham's problems. President John F. Kennedy was not really exaggerating much when he said later that "the civil rights movement owes 'Bull' Connor as much as it owes Abraham Lincoln."

Two specific results came of the Birmingham riots. After moderates among the white community saw the photographs of police dogs snarling at Negro children, they began to take steps to improve race relations within the city. And the same photographs did much to inspire planning for one of the most impressive political demonstrations ever held anywhere. It was the March on Washington, held on August 28, 1963, the one-hundredth anniversary of the Emancipation Proclamation.

More than a quarter of a million people, Negroes and whites, gathered in

At the foot of the Lincoln Memorial, Dr. King tells thousands of listeners: "I have a dream . . ."

Washington on that day to show their fervent support for the civil-rights bill then pending before Congress. Martin Luther King was only one of a long list of speakers who stood at the foot of the Lincoln Memorial and faced a sea of faces. But his were the words that stirred hearts the most. He spoke simply, and his words held listeners spellbound.

"I have a dream," Dr. King said. "I have a dream that one day this nation will rise up and live out the true meaning of its creed: 'We hold these truths to be self-evident, that all men are created equal.'

"I have a dream. . . . It is a dream firmly rooted in the American dream. I have a dream that one day in the red hills of Georgia, sons of former slaves and sons of former slave owners will be able to sit down together at the table of brotherhood. . . ."

Again and again Dr. King cried out: "I have a dream . . ." And each dream was a vision that some familiar phrase from the Declaration of Independence or the Constitution had come to apply to all Americans.

It was not only Americans who listened to Dr. King on that day. All over the world his words were relayed, and the people who heard them knew that the United States was moving toward its goal of equality for all Americans.

Dr. King's vital role in this progress was recognized the following year, when he received the Nobel Prize for Peace. The Swedish prize is given once a year to the individual anywhere in the world who has done most for "the furtherance of brotherhood among men."

Martin Luther King Jr. was thirty-

An important step forward in civil rights—the signing of the Civil Rights Bill of 1964 by President Lyndon B. Johnson.

five years old when he won the Nobel Peace Prize in 1964; he was the youngest man ever to be so honored since the award had been established in 1901. Because he demonstrated a new kind of heroism to all the world, he had been singled out in this remarkable way. But Dr. King himself took a more modest view of the honor.

It was, he said, "a tribute to the . . . majestic courage of gallant Negroes and white persons of good will who have followed a nonviolence course in seeking to establish a reign of justice and a rule of love across this nation of ours."

Despite his comparative youth, the Nobel Prize turned Dr. King into a sort of elder statesman of the Negro movement in the United States. Other voices, advocating a more militant civil-rights struggle, have disputed his counsel. But incomplete as it still is, the story of Martin Luther King Jr. has already become one of the foundation stones upon which Negro and white Americans are striving to build a color-blind society for the future.

HELEN KELLER
Symbol of Hope

Helen Keller was born on June 27, 1880, in Tuscumbia, Alabama. She said "tea, tea, tea" when she was only six months old and started to walk on her first birthday. Soon she was running to greet her father when he walked home from the offices of *The North Alabamian,* which he edited. She played with her mother in the rose garden surrounded by boxwood hedges.

For the first twenty months of her life, she had a completely normal childhood.

Then, in February 1882, four months before her second birthday, a sudden high fever put her in bed. The doctors called it congestion of the stomach and brain, but nobody really knew what it was. They said she could not live very long. As she tossed with pain on her bed, her mother soothed her. And then, as suddenly as it had come, the fever went.

Young Helen awoke and found the world was dark and still. She thought it was night, but the daylight never came. She wondered why it was so quiet, but the normal sounds of the household never resumed. She was completely blind and deaf.

It is almost impossible for a person who sees and hears to comprehend the world of the blind and the deaf. To be blind is a great handicap, but if a blind person can hear he can communicate with those around him. To be deaf is also a great handicap, but if a deaf person can see he can make his way in the world. To be both blind and deaf is to be totally cut off from people and things.

Gradually Helen got used to the silence and the darkness. If she remembered having been able to talk, she soon forgot. But her mind did not cloud over completely. She worked out a few signs to communicate her wants to her mother. A shake of the head meant no; a nod, yes. A pull meant come; a push, go. If she wanted ice cream, she pretended to turn the handle of the ice-cream freezer and shiver.

But unable to communicate more than these simple wants, she sometimes kicked and screamed for hours in frustration. Agonizing about their child and what would become of her, her parents tried to make things easy by catering to her whims—by spoiling her. Relatives said that Helen was mentally defective and should be placed in an institution, but her mother and father would have none of that. They would not give up hope for Helen, who had been so bright and lively as a baby.

From the age of two, Helen lived in a dark and silent world.

They took her to Baltimore to see an eye doctor, but he offered no hope. Why didn't they consult Dr. Alexander Graham Bell, one of the world's leading authorities on teaching the deaf? Everyone knew Dr. Bell. It had been his experiments in trying to aid the deaf that led to the invention of the telephone. Dr. Bell, in turn, suggested that the Perkins Institute in Boston might be able to furnish a teacher for Helen.

Mrs. Keller had read Charles Dickens' description of the Perkins Institute in his book *American Notes*. It was there that Dr. Samuel Gridley Howe had first bridged the chasm between the outside world and a person both blind and deaf. Using raised letters on cards, he had taught Laura Bridgman, who like Helen had lost her sight and hearing as a child, to understand and to communicate.

And so it was that Helen Keller was born again. The day was March 3, 1887, about three months before her seventh birthday. The afternoon sun shone through the honeysuckle and fell on Helen's face as she waited on the porch of her house in Alabama. From the bustle of the household, she had somehow sensed that something important was going to happen.

As she waited there, Helen Keller looked like a little savage. Her brown hair fell uncombed about her face, her black shoes were tied with white strings, her dress was dirty. She was a big girl for her age, with a ruddy complexion.

And she acted like a savage when a strange young woman approached. Helen rushed at her, almost bowling her over. Grabbing the stranger's pocketbook, she tried to open it, hoping to find candy. She flew into a rage when she couldn't find any.

The stranger was named Annie Sullivan. Only twenty years old and partially blind herself, she had been raised in a poorhouse in Massachusetts, where the insane had also been kept. But she had a fierce drive to learn and was sent to the Perkins Institute. Laura Bridgman taught her the manual alphabet, a system of spelling words by using fingers on someone else's palm. Then a series of operations partially restored her sight. Annie Sullivan graduated at the top of the class and this was her first job.

Although she was inexperienced as a teacher, Miss Sullivan knew that her biggest problem was how to control Helen, how to tame the savage child, without breaking her spirit.

"I shall go rather slowly at first and try to win her love," she wrote.

One of the first things that shocked her was Helen's appalling table manners. Spoiled by her parents, Helen was used to having her own way. At the dinner table, she would snatch food from platters and from other people's plates. Miss Sullivan decided that this could not continue.

Within a very few days, she stopped Helen from grabbing food from her teacher's plate. Helen promptly got down on the floor, screaming and kicking, a tactic that usually worked for her. After locking the dining-room door to make sure Helen could not run out, Miss Sullivan proceeded to eat her breakfast, although the food almost choked her.

Helen then tried another tactic. She pinched Miss Sullivan, who calmly slapped her. After a while, Helen sat down at the table. Miss Sullivan gave her a spoon; Helen threw it on the floor. Miss Sullivan grasped the child's hand and forced her to pick up the spoon. After this scene was repeated a few times, Helen finally kept the spoon and began to eat.

But the fight broke out again when the meal was over. Helen threw her napkin to the floor. Miss Sullivan made her pick it up. The battle of wills went on for more than an hour before Helen folded her napkin properly and left it on the table. Miss Sullivan opened the door and let Helen out.

Miss Sullivan confided the story to a friend in a letter that night and said: "I suppose I shall have many such battles with the little woman before she learns the only two essential things I can teach her, love and obedience."

She was right. That was only the first of many fights between the two strong-willed persons, the teacher and the pupil. Miss Sullivan was convinced that obedience was the gateway through which knowledge and love would enter the mind of the child. Patiently but firmly, she convinced Helen that temper tantrums would not work. In three weeks, the wild creature was transformed into a comparatively gentle child.

Then Helen began to learn. Repeatedly Miss Sullivan spelled out words onto Helen's palm. Quick to grasp the letters, Helen had some difficulty in understanding what the combination of letters meant.

While washing one morning, she pointed to the water in the basin and patted Miss Sullivan's hand. It was her way of asking a question. What was it? Miss Sullivan grasped the opportunity and brought Helen to the water pump.

With one hand, Helen held her mug under the pump as the cold water gushed out while Miss Sullivan spelled out w-a-t-e-r onto the other hand. Helen dropped her mug and stood quietly, obviously thinking. A light flashed over her face.

She reached for Miss Sullivan's hand and spelled back w-a-t-e-r. She had made the connection; she now knew that everything had a name and that the manual alphabet was the key to learning about all the things she wanted to know.

Eagerly, she pointed directly at Miss Sullivan. T-e-a-c-h-e-r was slowly spelled into her hand. She pointed at herself.

H-e-l-e-n was spelled. Before the day was over, Helen had learned thirty words.

That night for the first time, Helen crept into Miss Sullivan's bed and kissed her. "I thought my heart would burst, so full was it of joy," Miss Sullivan wrote.

Before long, Mrs. Keller said: "Miss Annie, I thank God every day of my life for sending you to us." And many years later, on her seventy-fifth birthday, Helen Keller said: "My birthday can never mean as much to me as the arrival of Annie Sullivan on March 3, 1887. That was my soul's birthday."

From that day forward, there was no stopping Helen Keller—and her remarkable teacher, Annie Sullivan. Helen learned to read Braille, the system of writing with raised dots on paper. She learned to "hear" by placing her fingers on the lips of people talking. She learned to write by using paper on top of a grooved board, with the grooves taking the place of lines. But she was not content; there was so much in the world, waiting for her.

"I must speak," she told Miss Sullivan, by spelling the letters onto her hand.

Off they went then to the Horace Mann School for the Deaf in Boston, where Sarah Fuller, the principal, became her teacher. The method was this: Helen's fingers passed lightly over Miss Fuller's face, jaws, mouth, teeth and even tongue, as Miss Fuller spoke. Imitating the position of the lips and tongue, Helen tried to repeat the sounds. Patiently she practiced until she learned the six elements of speech, P,M,S,A,T,I.

Her first sentence was: "It is warm." Even though it was indistinct, it was a triumph. She could speak.

Helen and Annie "talk" in the garden.

"I am not dumb now," she told Miss Sullivan, after her tenth lesson.

Nothing now seemed impossible for Helen Keller. As she grew into her teens, her desire for more education grew too. No longer was it simply a matter of communicating with the people around her. She wanted to know and understand more. Once in her home in Tuscumbia, during a discussion of the tariff problem, she asked a question. You can't understand, she was told.

"How do you know I cannot understand?" she replied. "I have a good mind."

There was no question about Helen's mind in the next few years as she buckled down to prepare herself for college. She was determined to enter Radcliffe College. To pass her entrance examinations, she spent three years studying Greek and Roman History, Latin,

"Sir Thomas" was given to Helen by her classmates at Radcliffe.

French, German, Algebra and Geometry. Every word, every sentence, every formula, she read in Braille or had spelled out letter by letter by Miss Sullivan.

Then came the written examinations. Helen had to pass the same entrance tests as the other girls, the girls who could read and write and study by themselves. Using a typewriter, she took her examinations—and passed.

As the new century dawned in 1900, twenty-year-old Helen Keller entered Radcliffe in the fall. With Annie Sullivan at her side in every class, spelling out the words of the teachers, Helen went from classroom to classroom, keeping pace with the other girls. She could not take notes in class, so she remembered the lessons and typed them when she got home. Miss Sullivan "read" books to Helen for five hours a day.

For her English classes, Helen wrote themes based on her own life. In 1903, her book *The Story of My Life* was published, recording her successful struggle to overcome her physical handicaps. The book was translated into fifty languages.

In 1904 Helen graduated from Radcliffe, with honors in English and German. When her name was called out at the graduating exercises, she climbed to the stage, hand in hand with Miss Sullivan, while the audience broke into thunderous applause.

One of her fellow graduates commented that Miss Sullivan deserved the degree equally. Helen was the first to agree. Her life and that of Annie Sullivan were intertwined. And soon after graduation, a third person joined them —a man, John Macy. He had been one of the friends who helped Helen with her book. He had fallen in love with Annie Sullivan.

Torn between her love for John and her love and responsibility for Helen, Miss Sullivan hesitated. But Helen insisted that she would not come between them, and so they were married. From then on the three of them lived together, with Annie Sullivan Macy continuing as the eyes and ears of Helen Keller.

Helen was determined to earn her own living. As the author of a popular book, she thought that the obvious way was by writing and lecturing. She could speak about her blindness and how it was overcome, but first she would have to make her harsh-sounding voice more pleasing. Not being able to hear it herself, she had fallen into the habit of using

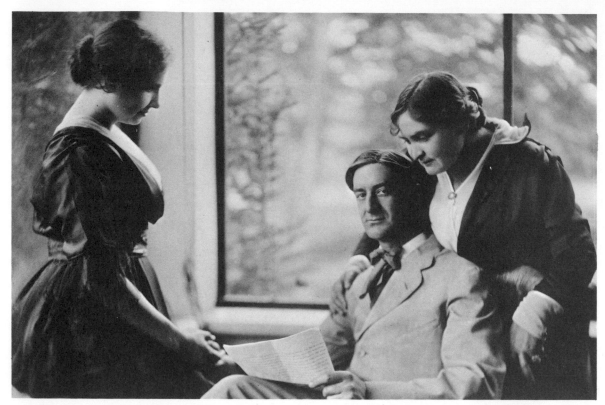

Helen with John Macy and Annie Sullivan.

a grating, unpleasant tone. So she went back to school for voice training.

She lectured and wrote for years. Her views on marriage, woman's suffrage and other issues of the day were sought after. Presidents and politicians, as well as lesser-known men and women everywhere, wanted to meet Miss Keller, the woman who had overcome such tremendous handicaps. With her teacher at her side, she talked about her handicaps and answered questions, always in good humor.

"Do you close your eyes when you sleep?" someone asked her.

"I never stayed awake to see," she replied.

The world's interest in Helen Keller has never died. A legend in her own time, she became a symbol of hope to the handicapped everywhere. It was not merely because she had overcome her own disabilities, which was a tremendous

accomplishment, but also because she had become a person whose thoughts and opinions were valued by thinking people throughout the world.

"I have often thought," she once wrote, "that it would be a blessing if every human being were stricken blind and deaf for a few days at a time during his early adult life. Darkness would make him more appreciative of sight, silence would teach him the joys of sound."

In 1920, Miss Keller decided that it was time to focus her energies on one major objective, aid for the blind. From then on, she devoted all her time and energy to help raise money for the American Foundation for the Blind. She and Mrs. Macy traveled around the world after John Macy's death, meeting kings and prime ministers, artists and musicians, people from all walks of life, who regarded these two as a shining ex-

34

ample of courage in the face of adversity.

Helen Keller's courage was deeply tested in 1936, when Mrs. Macy, her beloved teacher, died. Miss Keller wrote a book about her, called simply *Teacher*, in which she said:

"There was such virtue and power of communication in Teacher's personality that after her death I was emboldened to persevere in seeking new ways to give life and yet more life to other men and women in darkness and silence. Teacher believed in me and I resolved not to betray her faith."

With the aid of Polly Thompson, her secretary, who replaced Annie Sullivan Macy as her eyes and ears, Miss Keller continued her travels and her work. In World War II, just as she had in the First World War, she visited hospitals and, by her example, held out hope for blinded and other wounded soldiers.

Despite her advancing years, she would not rest. She once said: "I thank God for my handicaps, for through them, I have found myself, my work and my God." Finally, at the age of seventy-nine, she gave up traveling and stayed close to her home in Connecticut, reading, writing and thinking.

But the world has never forgotten her. She has received many honors from colleges and foreign nations. The United States Senate passed a resolution citing her tireless devotion to the handicapped. Governors of many states declared Helen Keller days in her honor. President Johnson spoke for all the peoples of the world in 1964 when he awarded the Medal of Freedom, America's highest civilian award, to Helen Keller "for her example of courage to all mankind."

President Eisenhower's smile delighted Helen Keller.

DOUGLAS MacARTHUR
"I Shall Return"

Four PT boats slipped out of Manila Bay in the darkness, riding low in the choppy water. Ahead was the Japanese fleet, patrolling the coast of the Philippine Islands. All those aboard the small American craft stood watch tensely, waiting for a burst of shellfire which would mark their discovery, and which must surely mean death or capture. But nothing happened. The little flotilla passed by the Japanese warships and headed south.

Gaunt in his war-stained uniform, General Douglas MacArthur raised his cap then in a farewell salute to the American and Philippine troops he had to leave behind. It was March 11, 1942. For nearly three months his men had desperately resisted overwhelming attacks by the Japanese, until their backs had been pushed to the sea at Bataan and Corregidor. Over his own objections, the general had just been ordered by President Franklin D. Roosevelt to leave his battered troops and the Philippine people, whom he had sworn to defend. With a heavy heart, he was following the orders; his wife, his four-year-old son and some key aides accompanied him.

A colorful as well as a controversial figure, with many enthusiastic admirers —and, it sometimes seemed, nearly as many equally enthusiastic critics—MacArthur arrived in Australia to find it bracing for an attack by the advancing Japanese. He was noted as a stirring speaker, a master of publicity. Now he proved the reputation was deserved. Although he well knew he had only a pitiful amount of equipment and only a few trained men at his disposal, he immediately struck a dramatic note that echoed all around the world.

"The President of the United States ordered me to . . . proceed from Corregidor to Australia," he proclaimed on landing. "I came through and *I shall return.*"

Those three words, "I shall return," instantly became a rallying cry for the Australians, a glowing beacon of hope for those in the Philippines. Still there were many who thought the general's bold promise could not possibly be kept. In those spring days of 1942, the tide of Japanese conquest seemed invincible. Soon after December 7, 1941, when the Japanese had bombed Pearl Harbor, plunging the United States into war, the attackers had also invaded the Netherlands East Indies, Malaya, Singapore and other British, French and Dutch posses-

Douglas MacArthur (center) first displayed personal courage and military talent as a leader of the Rainbow Division.

sions in Southeast Asia. Almost everywhere the Japanese were still advancing relentlessly, and the Allied forces appeared powerless to stop them.

Now the defense of the Southwest Pacific was being placed in the hands of Douglas MacArthur. At the age of sixty-one, he was the most famous, most flamboyant, most decorated and, some said, the best general in the United States Army. His sternly handsome face had been pictured on front pages everywhere. His corn-cob pipe and his elaborately braided Army cap, worn with studied carelessness, were familiar to newspaper readers around the world.

The son of a general—General Arthur MacArthur, who had also won fame in the Philippines, during and after the Spanish-American War of 1898—Douglas MacArthur had had his mind set on a soldier's career from his earliest boyhood. Almost from his birth, on January 26, 1880, on an Army base near Little Rock, Arkansas, he seemed set on winning a general's stars on his own; it was his great thirst for glory that many people held against him. Yet even his enemies had to admit that he earned the honors that came to him.

At West Point, Douglas MacArthur stood out. He was captain of the corps of cadets when he graduated in 1903, and he also had an outstanding scholastic record. But it was not until World War I that he first distinguished himself in the eyes of the American public at large. Then he helped to organize the Rainbow Division, and although he was among the youngest generals in the Army, he commanded one of its brigades.

By his brilliant planning of how to make the best possible use of available troops and by his daring in personally leading raids on enemy positions, he won swift promotion—and one medal after another. No armchair general, he once spent four days and four nights without sleep, pressing after retreating Germans. When World War I ended, he had received the prized Silver Star medal five times, and he had *two* Distinguished Service Crosses.

With the coming of peace, MacArthur was assigned to go back to West Point, this time as its commander. On the basis of his battlefield experience, he completely revamped the course of study at the military academy. Then in 1930 he was called to Washington to fill the highest post the Army could offer. As Chief of Staff during the Depression years, when the army of unemployed was more on the nation's mind than was its uniformed soldiery, MacArthur had little success in his constant efforts to keep civilian law-makers from cutting military funds.

In 1935, he retired from this budgetary fray, going on inactive status to accept the task of helping the Philippines organize defenses against the growing threat of Japanese aggression. Early in 1941, when war clouds were getting more ominous, MacArthur was recalled to active duty in the United States Army. His mission: to build a combined American and Filipino defense network in the Philippines. But before the job was done, Japanese warplanes began dropping bombs.

During those despairing days of defeat in the spring of 1942, MacArthur acted in Australia on his firm belief that a good offense is the best defense. He immediately began to plan for his return to the Philippines. He demanded more men and more equipment, not concealing his disagreement with the grand strategy of President Franklin D. Roosevelt, Prime Minister Winston Churchill of England and his own superior in the Army, Chief of Staff George C. Marshall. The Allied strategists had agreed that they would fight to defeat Germany first, while holding the line in the Pacific.

But a mere holding operation could not satisfy MacArthur. He wanted to move Australia's first line of defense to the north—to the rugged, mountainous island of New Guinea. The tentacles of Japanese conquest were slowly moving down the northern coast of New Guinea toward Australia. MacArthur thought it would be suicidal to wait for them. Instead he rushed all his available troops into New Guinea. In the jungles and swamps of that primitive island, MacArthur attacked the overextended Japanese lines and stopped the Japanese advance.

By-passing enemy strongpoints and concentrating on cutting their lines of supply, MacArthur isolated the Japanese on New Guinea. He left those who remained to starve or scrounge for supplies. This technique reversed the course of the war in the South Pacific. Meanwhile, farther to the east, American marines and soldiers attacked at Guadalcanal, starting the rollback of the Japanese from another direction.

Step by step in 1943 and 1944, the American forces—under MacArthur in the Southwest Pacific and under Admiral Chester Nimitz in the South Pacific—island-hopped toward the Philippines. By late 1944, it was clear that the ever-growing American military power could be used sooner than Washington had expected. Why not an immediate invasion of the Philippines?

MacArthur knew the assault would be difficult; the Japanese would fight doggedly to retain the islands, knowing that the Philippines would be the springboard for the invasion of Japan itself. Nevertheless, MacArthur pressed for action.

On October 19–20, 1944, a force of 174,000 American fighting men, supported by 700 ships of the Navy, converged on Leyte Gulf in the Philippines.

General MacArthur (second from left) wading ashore with his staff at Leyte Gulf.

At dawn the big guns of the battleships roared. Under their protection, landing craft loaded with infantrymen churned their way to the sandy beaches. With the third wave of troops, Douglas MacArthur waded ashore and stood once more on Philippine soil.

"People of the Philippines, I have returned," he said into a microphone connected with a mobile broadcasting unit, which would beam his words throughout the islands.

"By the grace of Almighty God, our forces stand again on Philippine soil—soil consecrated by the blood of our two peoples. We have come dedicated and committed to the task of destroying every vestige of enemy control of your daily lives and of restoring a foundation of indestructible strength, the liberties of your people."

Heavy fighting remained before the liberation of the islands was completed, but Leyte was conquered in a brief period. Then the American forces landed near Manila, duplicating the invasion by the Japanese three years earlier. This time it was the American forces that quickly overcame the defenders; this time the triumph led to the opening of prison gates. Thousands of Americans, feeble from hunger, were freed from Japanese prison camps. Even as these survivors were rejoicing at their liberation from months and years of horror, American generals and admirals were starting to plan for the next step—the conquest of Japan itself.

America accepts the formal surrender of Japan as MacArthur signs the peace treaty.

Surrender or be destroyed: this ultimatum went out to Japan in the summer of 1945. When no answer came, the American Air Force Superfort the *Enola Gay* on August 6 dropped the first atomic bomb in history on the Japanese industrial city of Hiroshima. Hiroshima was devastated. President Harry S. Truman once again demanded the surrender of Japan, but again there was no response. On August 9, a second atomic bomb exploded, destroying the city of Nagasaki. The following day, Japan surrendered.

Then General Douglas MacArthur was appointed Supreme Commander for the Allied Powers, to accept the surrender.

With his usual daredevil courage,

MacArthur disregarded warnings about dissident Japanese and flew into Japan with a handful of aides. His corn-cob pipe jutted jauntily from his mouth as he landed at Atsugi Airport outside Yokohama. Then he rode fifteen miles to the city, down a route lined by a guard of armed Japanese soldiers. MacArthur set September 2, 1945, as the date for the formal surrender and the quarterdeck of the U.S.S. *Missouri* as the scene of the ceremony.

On that historic day, representatives of the Emperor of Japan came aboard the American warship and signed the surrender agreement. MacArthur waited until they had finished, then said: "Let us pray that peace be now restored to the world and that God will preserve it always."

The proceedings had ended, the war was over, American and Allied troops by the thousands could return home. But a remarkable phase in the career of Douglas MacArthur was just starting, for he had accepted a staggering challenge. As commander of America's force occupying the conquered nation, he undertook to lead his former enemies onto an entirely new path—the path toward democracy.

Until the surrender the Emperor of Japan had, in theory at least, exercised absolute power over his subjects; in practice, a small group of power-hungry military men ruled the country. The collapse of their ambitious schemes for dominating the Far East left the Japanese people bewildered and miserable. A new awareness that they were hated by much of the rest of the world only added to the problems left in the wake of the war's destruction. And the Japanese were a proud people, unable to accept the view that their own ways were all wrong; in particular, they clung to their reverence for their Emperor.

These were the conditions faced by General MacArthur as he began his efforts to democratize Japan.

First he saw to it that the Japanese war leaders were stripped of all authority. They were tried, convicted and punished as war criminals. But in this and other actions, MacArthur showed a tact and restraint that vastly increased the respect in which he was held, both at home and abroad. As a matter of cold fact, the American general held more power than even the Japanese Emperor had enjoyed before the war. Yet MacArthur did not bluster or order the Japanese to follow his commands. Instead he sought the Emperor's cooperation and, working within the framework of the imperial government, gradually moved Japan in the direction of freedom.

For the next five years, General MacArthur fostered the modernizing of Japan's constitution, the holding of free elections, the establishing of labor unions. Little by little Japan, the former enemy of the United States, was transformed into a friend and close ally, as well as a respected member of the community of free nations.

Looking back at the occupation period, MacArthur himself commented: "The pages of history in recording America's twentieth century contributions may, perchance, pass over lightly

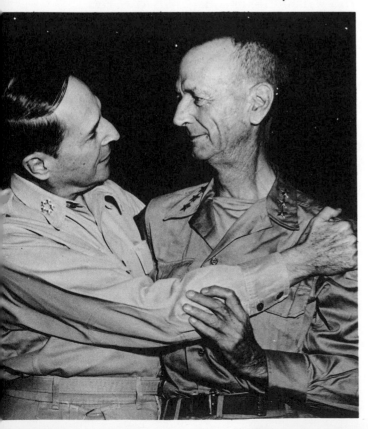

Thin and pale after three years in a Japanese prison camp, General Jonathan Wainwright is reunited with General MacArthur. Wainwright was captured after taking over MacArthur's command on Corregidor.

the wars we have fought. But I believe they will not fail to record the influence for good upon Asia which will inevitably follow the spiritual regeneration of Japan."

But the serenity of the American occupation of Japan was shattered on the morning of June 25, 1950. That day North Korean troops, armed and aided by the Soviet Union, swept across the thirty-eighth parallel and invaded South Korea, which was being protected by the United States.

In emergency session, the United Nations Security Council asked its members to support the Republic of South Korea in resisting the aggressors. Translated into practical terms, this mission fell to the United States. President Truman ordered General MacArthur to step into his military role once again and to save South Korea.

It was almost as if history were being repeated. Just as the Japanese had swept to early conquest, so now the North Korean Communist army swiftly drove down the Korean peninsula, brushing aside the South Korean defenders and the few American soldiers already on the scene. Time would be needed for the American pipeline of supplies and soldiers to provide massive assistance, and it seemed as if the North Koreans might achieve victory before the weight of America arrived. But the combined South Korean forces and contingents of occupation troops flown in from Japan managed to keep a tiny foothold around the southernmost South Korean city of Pusan.

MacArthur the strategist knew that he could not drive the North Koreans back on land except by a tremendous expenditure of men and arms, neither of which was available to him yet. Overriding the objections of Washington, he decided instead to land two divisions of Americans from the sea at the western Korean port of Inchon, just outside the South Korean capital of Seoul. This maneuver drove a wedge into the rear of the North Korean armies and they retreated in disorder. The victory, which restored all of South Korea to its elected government, was considered to be one of the most brilliant military strokes of modern times.

Unfortunately, however, MacArthur pressed his victory to the point of disaster. He divided his forces in half and sent them chasing the retreating Communists to the Yalu, the river that divides Korea from China. He believed that the war was practically over and that there was "very little" chance the Chinese would intervene. Indeed, he utterly ignored warnings that China would react to the presence of American troops at her border.

The Chinese struck in force just as the Americans reached the Yalu. Once more the defenders of South Korea retreated in haste; once more the Communists raced south and captured Seoul; once more the United Nations forces pushed their way back north. The battle stabilized in the neighborhood of the thirty-eighth parallel.

By this time, MacArthur had come to believe that the war could be won only by aircraft attacks on Chinese supply depots and on supply lines within China. But President Harry S. Truman held firmly to the position that a war with

China would be the wrong war, at the wrong place and at the wrong time.

Instead of passively accepting his Commander-in-Chief's views, MacArthur disputed them. In a letter to a friend in the United States, he wrote that "there is no substitute for victory." When the letter was published, President Truman acted.

"Military commanders must be governed by the policies and directives issued to them in the manner prescribed by our laws and Constitution," said the President. Asserting the nation's tradition of civilian rather than military control of its armed forces—one of the basic foundations of American democracy—

Truman stripped MacArthur of his command and ordered the 71-year-old general to come home.

General MacArthur received a hero's welcome when he arrived in the United States; it seemed there were many people who applauded his outspoken defiance of the President. Yet in the Washington hearings and debate that ensued, Mr. Truman's right to act as he had was strongly upheld.

In the end the issue was closed on a sentimental note. Speaking before a joint session of Congress, the general defended his actions in Korea, but concluded with a reference to the old military ballad

Truman and MacArthur discussing strategy during a meeting on Wake Island, 1951.

which holds that old soldiers never die, they just fade away.

"Like the old soldier of that ballad," said General MacArthur, "I now close my military career and fade away—an old soldier who tried to do his duty as God gave him the light to see that duty."

Thus fears that the general might lead an open fight against the President were dispelled, and the American people were free to demonstrate their affection for MacArthur as a man who had surely earned an honorable retirement. Even some of his severest critics joined in the crowds that turned out for MacArthur parades in many cities.

The general and his wife settled in the Waldorf-Astoria Hotel in New York. MacArthur became chairman of the board of the Remington-Rand Corporation and devoted much time to writing his memoirs. He died in New York on April 5, 1964, at the age of eighty-four, revered as a brilliant military leader, the architect of democracy in Japan—and a man of great personal courage.

RICHARD E. BYRD
Polar Explorer

Eleven-year-old Dick Byrd was ready to leave on his first real trip—and quite a trip it should be. From his home in Winchester, Virginia, he was on his way to the Philippine Islands, alone. His new suitcase was packed with clothing and other necessities, including a jackknife and a ball of string.

When friends of his family had invited him, his mother had, of course, objected. But he managed to win her consent. So in the summer of the exciting year of 1900, the year a new century was starting, the boy with a faraway look in his eyes began his first big adventure.

By train across the continent to San Francisco, Dick watched America unfold. Then, by steamer, he crossed the wide Pacific, stopping in Nagasaki, Japan, after riding out a Pacific typhoon. From the deck of his ship he watched the coast of China in the distance before finally landing in Manila.

He arrived there just in time to see the last stages of the Philippine Insurrection, when the Filipinos, liberated from Spain by the United States two years earlier, were attempting to gain their complete freedom. Dick even slipped away on a pony one day to join a posse of the mounted constabulary rounding

up a band of dangerous bandits.

When the time came to return home, Dick's thirst for adventure made him decide on a new course. Instead of merely retracing his route, he would keep on going westward around the world until he reached America.

By ship, he crossed the Indian Ocean, traversed the Suez Canal, proceeded on through the Mediterranean Sea and across the Atlantic Ocean to New York. Then, it was a short train trip from New York back home to Winchester.

Before his thirteenth birthday Dick Byrd had circumnavigated the globe. It was a most unusual trip, but he was a most unusual boy.

"Richard was born an adventurer and explorer, absolutely without fear," his mother said.

Back in the green valley of the Shenandoah, where memories of the battles between the blue-clad Union and the grey-coated Confederate armies still remained fresh, Dick began to dream of new worlds to conquer.

Dick and his two brothers came from a long line of soldiers and statesmen. The first Byrd had arrived in Virginia from England in the 1600's; his descendants established a pattern of public service that never was broken. The oldest of the three brothers, Harry, grew up to serve as governor of Virginia and a United States senator. Tom, the youngest, was decorated for action against the Germans in World War I. And Dick (christened Richard Evelyn Byrd when he was born on October 25, 1888) became one of the most famous explorers of the twentieth century.

His father, a distinguished lawyer, had planned a legal career for his middle son, but it soon became clear that Dick's interests lay elsewhere. After Admiral Robert E. Peary reached the North Pole in 1909, Dick wrote in his diary that he would go there, too.

Quiet and thoughtful, Dick was nevertheless the leader of the band of boys near home. No matter what the physical risk, he was always ready to go first when some new challenge arose. His parents called it "reckless deviltry"; others would later call it a capacity for leadership.

At the United States Naval Academy, which he entered in 1908, he demonstrated the same characteristics. He held more offices than any other midshipman during his four years there. He was one of the boldest players on the football team. Yet he never lost the dreamy look in his eyes. His classmates remembered the day he absent-mindedly forgot to salute the commandant, and the time he appeared in formation perfectly uniformed—except that he was wearing yellow civilian shoes.

A good student, Byrd was also an outstanding athlete. He played football until he broke his leg in a game. As captain of the gymnasium team, he broke the leg once more when he fell from the rings high above the gym floor in an attempt to perform a difficult feat. The bones never knit properly and these accidents probably helped determine the shape of his career.

When he graduated from the Academy in 1912, the yearbook said: "Most of the time Dick moves around with a far-away look in his eyes. . . . He has already lived a life rich in experience and he will live a life richer still."

Byrd served at sea for four years, but he was forced to retire from the Navy in 1916 because his injured leg weakened under the strain of standing long watches aboard ship.

A year later, when the United States entered World War I, Byrd returned to the service, but to a desk job that he detested. He wanted to fight, and he knew there was only one military job he could perform without the full use of his legs—flying.

"Give me a chance," he begged a medical board. "I want to fly. Give me a month of it and if I don't improve to suit you, I'll do anything you say."

He was given a month to prove his point. Off he went to the Naval Air Training Station at Pensacola, Florida. On his first day there, he watched a training plane plummet straight into the bay, killing both instructor and student.

"Want to go up?" one of the instructors asked him, as he watched the rescue party at work.

Byrd hesitated, but only for an instant. He put on flying goggles and a helmet and climbed aboard a plane. In those early days of flying, the planes were primitive and the flying techniques scarcely more advanced.

His instructor took off and, after flying for several minutes, pointed to the stick. Byrd suddenly realized that he had control of the plane. There was no time to argue. By using common sense, he managed to keep his course straight ahead, but the plane began to lose altitude fast. The instructor took over and brought them down safely.

For some it might have been a frightening experience, but Byrd liked it. He quickly mastered the principles of flying. After six hours of instruction, he made his first solo flight, earning his wings as a pilot. And, as he had hoped, his injured leg didn't bother him any more.

Having succeeded in convincing his superiors to allow him to fly, Byrd now turned his attention to getting to the combat area. He conceived of a project to deliver the Navy's largest plane—the NC flying boat, then almost completed —to Europe by flying across the Atlantic. With a two-man crew, he thought the unprecedented ocean crossing could open a new era in aviation.

"There is one thing, at least, which I can truly say of my career," Byrd wrote later. "It is that from the moment I became a full-fledged Navy pilot my ambition was to make a career in aviation. Not merely in the sense of routine flying, but rather in the pioneering sense."

The airplane had only recently been added to man's stock of tools, and Byrd aimed "to test the tool to its utmost."

Approval for the transatlantic flight came in 1919, after the war ended—but with it came a great disappointment for Byrd, the man who had thought of the trip. The orders were to let men who worked at desks during the war have the honor of making the flight; Byrd, who had served on a submarine-scouting air patrol off the coast of Canada, was therefore ineligible. But he was determined to make the flight succeed, even if he didn't fly himself.

On May 16 three huge flying boats, the NC-1, NC-3 and NC-4, took off from St. John's, Newfoundland; Byrd watched them out of sight. Two days later the reports came in: two of the planes had gone down over the water and their crews had been rescued by ships in the area and the third plane, the NC-4, had landed in the Azores. The NC-4 then flew on to Lisbon, completing the first transatlantic flight in history.

Convinced that his big chance for fame had passed him by, Byrd went back to routine jobs in the Navy. But he kept working for a bigger role for aviation within the ship-oriented service.

Another opportunity came in 1924, when the Navy planned a flight of the dirigible *Shenandoah* across the Arctic Ocean from Point Barrow, Alaska, to Spitzbergen, an island near the northern tip of Norway. In the midst of the preparations, the project was suddenly called off; but Byrd was determined to go ahead on his own with an even bolder plan for exploring in the polar region. He had never forgotten his boyhood ambition to see the North Pole—and now he aimed to fly over it. No man had yet accomplished this feat.

Within a year he had organized a small expedition, with the help of private funds and the National Geographic Society, to make some preliminary flights out of Greenland over Arctic lands and waters. The Navy cooperated by allowing the use of its planes. In these flights, he learned about the dangers of flying in frigid weather and found one of his main aides for the future—Floyd Bennett, who until then had been an obscure Naval aviation mechanic.

Back in the United States, Byrd and Bennett laid their plans for a flight over the North Pole. Technically on leaves of absence from the Navy, they set about organizing the expedition. Byrd selected for the flight a trimotored Fokker airplane, named the *Josephine Ford* after the three-year-old daughter of Edsel Ford, who made a large financial contribution to the expedition.

On April 5, 1926, Byrd, with sixty men and a six-month food supply, sailed out of the Brooklyn Navy Yard, bound for Spitzbergen. When they arrived there three weeks later, Byrd was stunned to discover a difficulty that had not been anticipated. A Norwegian ship was tied up at the only sizeable dock the little harbor boasted. Not only did Byrd have to anchor his own steamer offshore, amid dangerous floes of drift ice; he also had to improvise some sort of raft on which his heavy plane could be towed to the beach.

Norwegian seamen urged Byrd to give up any such idea. "You know nothing about ice, or you would not attempt such a thing," he was warned. "The ice is almost certain to start moving before you can get ashore." Then raft and plane both would be crushed.

But Byrd would not be deterred. By laying heavy planks across the gunwales of the steamer's four lifeboats, his crew constructed a makeshift raft big enough to carry the plane, which was 42 feet long with a wingspread of 63 feet. In the midst of a snow squall, the *Josephine Ford* was hoisted from the steamer's hold and lowered onto the raft.

"We were taking a tremendous chance in doing this," Byrd admitted later. Had a wind sprung up, the plane would surely have been lost. Yet he would not consider accepting defeat right at the outset.

Luck was with him, though, and he managed to get his men and his equipment onto land. Then the next problem was even more awesome. No such convenience as a smooth, snow-free runway could be expected, and the plan was to equip the *Josephine Ford* with skis before attempting a takeoff. But no one knew how efficiently a plane of this size would perform on skis.

Furthermore, there was no level stretch long enough to serve as a runway. "We were forced to try another new stunt—to take off going downhill," Byrd reported later.

Three times Byrd and Bennett got set for a test flight, and each time the plane failed to take off and floundered into a snowdrift. Skis were broken to bits, the landing gear was bent and broken. Working day and night in below zero temperatures, carpenters connected with the expedition fashioned new skis and repaired the plane. When the next take-off attempt succeeded, final preparations were made for the polar flight. Shortly after midnight on May 9, the two men raced their plane down the runway. Emergency supplies of fuel and food made it so heavy that the chances for getting off the ground safely seemed slight. But at the last possible second the plane lurched up into the air, then headed due north.

Looking somewhat like polar bears in their fur boots and parkas, Byrd and Bennett took turns piloting and navigating. It was 720 miles to their destination, and to find it would be no easy task. Because the magnetic north pole was about a thousand miles south of the geographic North Pole, navigating instruments could not be relied on. The sun, constantly shining since this was summer in the Arctic, was their best guide over the frozen wasteland where scores of men had died in attempts to reach the North Pole via dogsled.

Despite the constant peril of frostbite —twice Byrd felt his face stiffening and had to rub the circulation back—the flight was comparatively uneventful for the first several hours. Then a bad leak developed in the oil tank of the starboard motor. "That motor will stop," Bennett wrote on a pad (because of the noise of the motors, they could not hear each other speak). Then he suggested an emergency landing, so they could try to fix the leak.

Byrd shook his head.

A forced landing would be extremely dangerous. And if they were on course, they were only about an hour from the Pole. Byrd always said he was not superstitious, but inside a pocket of his shirt was a coin Admiral Peary had carried on his successful search for the North Pole; perhaps because of the coin, Dick Byrd decided to ignore the oil leak.

His decision proved historic. At 9:02 A.M. on May 9, 1926, his calculations showed them to be at the Pole. Beneath them was, as Byrd wrote later, "a great

Commander Byrd (left) with Floyd Bennett before their takeoff for the North Pole in 1926.

eternally frozen, snow-covered ocean, broken into ice fields or cakes of various sizes and shapes." For thirteen minutes they circled the Pole, before turning back to Spitzbergen.

And luck was still with them. Every instant they expected one motor to stop. "But, to our astonishment, a miracle was happening," Byrd wrote later. He discovered afterward that the oil-tank leak was caused by a rivet that had jarred out of its hole; when the oil had gone down to the level of the hole it had stopped leaking out.

Byrd came back to the United States a hero. He was not the first person to reach the pole, of course; Admiral Peary had earned that honor back in 1909. But the pioneering flight over the Pole captured the imagination of the American public. Byrd was promoted to the rank of commander in the Navy. He received the

51

nation's Medal of Honor and the National Geographic Society's Hubbard Medal. He was also overwhelmed by a ticker-tape parade up Broadway; with Floyd Bennett at his side, he was showered with confetti and streamers.

But Byrd was not thinking of "this hero business," as he put it; already he was planning his next expedition, the fulfillment of a dream that had started many years before—a flight across the Atlantic Ocean. He had planned the NC flight back in 1919; but that had been accomplished in easy stages—from New York to Nova Scotia to the Azores to Europe. This flight would be nonstop across the ocean, New York to Paris; with a copilot and a "payload" of mail sacks, to prove that transatlantic air service was a practical possibility.

Once again, Byrd rounded up private capital to back the flight. Once again, he planned to use a three-engined plane, this time one called the *America*. He made a test flight on April 20, 1927, but the plane crashed on landing. Bennett, again his copilot, was severely injured; Byrd's arm was broken.

Not daunted, Byrd proceeded with his plans. The plane was rebuilt and the crew planned to take off on May 21. Two thousand persons gathered at Roosevelt Field for the christening of the *America*.

As the speeches began, they were interrupted by a news flash. Lindbergh had landed in Paris; he had flown the Atlantic all by himself in a single-engined plane. "The Lone Eagle" had beaten Byrd to Paris.

Disappointed but determined not to interfere with Lindbergh's triumph, Byrd postponed his flight. It wasn't until

June 29 that he took off, accompanied by Bernt Balchen, Bert Acosta and George O. Noville.

They flew to Nova Scotia, over the station where Byrd had served in the First World War, and from then on the weather could not have been worse. The fog was so thick they could see neither land nor water; the sun, the moon, the stars, all their possible navigational guides, were completely hidden.

"I have seen neither land or sea since three o'clock yesterday. Everything completely covered by fog," Byrd radioed more than twenty-four hours later.

From time to time the men received radio messages from ships at sea. They kept flying ahead, unsure of where they would come out of the fog. On the second day, as darkness fell, they passed over the coastline of France. They had made it; they had crossed the ocean successfully, following in Lindbergh's tracks.

The men relaxed. They thought the rest of the trip would be easy; Paris was dead ahead. But when their calculations indicated that they had arrived there, they could see nothing. Fog completely covered the Paris area.

With his gas running out, Byrd made a quick decision. He would head back for the coast and ditch the plane in the ocean. "At least we shall kill no one but ourselves," he said.

Balchen, the pilot, put the plane down into the water. With a terrific roar, the landing gear was torn off and the plane crashed. Bruised, tired and watersoaked, the four men rescued the mail bags, pumped up a rubber boat and paddled to shore.

Despite their failure to land in Paris, Byrd and his crew were greeted as heroes in France, and, for the second time, in New York later. And once again in the midst of celebration, Byrd was thinking ahead to the new challenge—which would be the last and greatest of his career—the South Pole.

Antarctica still remained a geographical mystery. Was it a continent? Or was it, like the Arctic, an ocean covered with ice and snow? At the Pole itself was a vast ice plateau nearly two miles high, but what was beneath it?

Antarctica had been discovered in 1840 by a United States Navy expedition commanded by John Wilkes, but the exploration of the area had not really started until the dawn of the twentieth century. Only two expeditions had yet reached the South Pole.

Roald Amundsen, a Norwegian, had arrived there on December 14, 1911, by dog sled; and just as important, he returned safely. The loser in the race to the Pole, Robert Falcon Scott, an English naval officer and explorer, reached the Pole area in January of 1912 and, to his bitter disappointment, found evidence that Amundsen had been there

At Little America, with the temperature at 64 degrees below zero, Admiral Byrd's men melt snow for drinking water.

first. Lacking adequate supplies, Scott and his party died on the return trip, but records of their discovery of Amundsen's tents were later found.

Like most successful explorers, Byrd had learned that careful preparation was the secret to success. Even though he was a Naval officer, his expeditions were private affairs, organized by him and financed by private organizations and individuals; the United States Government, although interested, took no official part. Byrd bought his ships, stocked them, organized his manpower and assumed full responsibility for the lives of his men and the success of their endeavors.

In late 1928 he sailed for the Antarctic, establishing a camp there on December 30. "It is as quiet here as a tomb," Byrd wrote in his diary. "Nothing stirs. The silence is so deep, one could almost reach out and touch it."

After unloading, Byrd and his men set about on their major job of scientific observation. They made many important discoveries, among them two major mountain ranges; he named them the Edsel Ford Mountains and the Rockefeller Mountains (honoring sponsors of his expedition). He also called one area Marie Byrd Land for his wife. And he established a base, Little America. But all this was overshadowed by his one main goal: flying to the South Pole.

He was ready on November 29, 1929. With a three-man crew, consisting of Bernt Balchen as the pilot, Harold I. June as copilot, and Captain Ashley C. McKinley as the photographer, Byrd took off in a plane he had named the *Floyd Bennett* in honor of his North Pole pilot, who had died of pneumonia the year before.

Flying over the route that Amundsen had pioneered—at a maximum speed of about one mile an hour—the *Floyd Bennett* soared along at about ninety miles an hour.

At an altitude of about 9,600 feet, the plane approached the two-mile-high plateau at the Pole. To keep from crashing, the plane would have to be lightened. Which should be sacrificed, gasoline or food? Byrd ordered the bags of food thrown overboard.

The plane climbed then, above the endless stretches of white. There was nothing on the ground below to indicate the imaginary point where all the meridians of longitude converge, but at 1:14 in the afternoon, Byrd decided on the basis of his navigational calculations that they had arrived. They were above the South Pole.

Opening the trap door of the plane, he dropped a small American flag weighted with stone from Floyd Bennett's grave. Then he radioed the news of arrival back to Little America.

When Byrd returned to the United States after this mission, a grateful Congress promoted him to the rank of rear admiral in the Navy. He collected more medals; and as was his habit, he planned more trips. The Antarctic was to remain his objective for the rest of his life.

In 1933 he set out once more for Little America and mapped more of the unknown continent; he even spent four months of the fierce Antarctic winter entirely alone at an advance-base weather station, recording temperature, wind velocity and other measurements. Despite a series of mishaps that almost killed him—he injured a shoulder while carrying heavy equipment, and then was almost poisoned by a faulty gas heater in his tunnel shelter—he refused to radio word of his condition back to Little America; any rescue attempt before the severe blizzard season ended would acutely endanger other lives. After recovering his health, he led a third Antarctic expedition in 1939.

Byrd saw active service in the Navy in World War II, and then returned to the Antarctic twice more, in 1946–47 and in 1955. Both of these expeditions were under official Navy auspices and carried out extensive mapping, meteorological and other scientific projects.

The latter expedition, known as Operation Deep Freeze, launched America's strong Antarctic contribution to the International Geophysical Year (IGY). This period of international cooperation in scientific research was scheduled to begin in July 1957. During the planning stages, Admiral Byrd helped to focus American interest on Antarctica, where conditions were at first thought to be too severe for a major research effort.

Named head of the American Antarctic programs, Byrd led Operation Deep Freeze in selecting sites and building bases for the IGY scientists. Now Byrd had the use of helicopters, huge planes and heavy tractors for his work; the days of dog sleds and rickety planes were over.

For Byrd, perhaps the most significant aspect of the IGY activities in Antarctica was the opportunity for peaceful cooperation among the twelve nations—free

and Communist—planning to send expeditions there. Byrd called Antarctica "the great white continent of peace," and he was anxious to see it remain so. He promoted the adoption of an international treaty outlawing nuclear weapons in Antarctica, but did not live to see its signing in 1961.

No longer a boy with a faraway look in his eyes, Admiral Byrd died in 1957. During his sixty-eight years, he had seen more of the globe than almost anybody else. He had dauntlessly explored both polar regions, and he had shared his findings by writing books about his major expeditions. He had also attained his aim and gained a high rank among aviation's pioneers, as well as a sure place in the company of American heroes.

A gesture for peace in Antarctica: Admiral Byrd preparing to drop the flags of the United Nations over the South Pole.

GORDON SEAGRAVE
Burma Surgeon

A five-year-old boy sat on his porch in Rangoon, listening to the tales of a tall doctor. The boy was American, but Rangoon in far-off Burma was his home; he had been born there on March 18, 1897. His great-grandfather had come halfway around the world from the United States many years earlier to serve as a missionary.

Entranced, the boy listened to the visitor. Then the tall doctor began doing tricks. First he grasped the back of a chair with his teeth—and without using his hands at all, lifted the chair up over his head.

The little boy tried the same trick himself, using his small nursery chair, but it didn't work.

The doctor next asked for a glass of water. After the boy fetched it, that remarkable man carefully stood on his head. And, upside down, he drank the glass of water!

The boy was speechless with awe. When the man had gone, he hurried to ask his mother who the visitor had been.

"He is Dr. Robert Harper," his mother told him. She added that Dr. Harper was a medical missionary at Namkham, on the border between the northern Shan States and China.

Without hesitation the boy said:

"When I grow up, I'm going to be a medical missionary in the Shan States." Thus Gordon Stifler Seagrave settled the matter of his career.

Of course the decision was not quite that simple. In years to come, he liked to tell people that watching Dr. Harper's entertaining tricks had made up his mind. But his own family's example deserved more credit.

For three generations, his family had dedicated their lives to serving others less fortunate. His great-grandfather, his grandfather, his parents and several aunts and uncles had all chosen to give up the comfort of life in the United States in favor of teaching in primitive schools in Burmese villages. Their selfless zeal came from their belief that bringing word of the Christian religion to this distant land would save many souls. Young Gordon Seagrave shared the devout Baptist convictions of his missionary relatives—but he also aimed to heal bodily sickness.

Nevertheless, Gordon was a spirited boy. One day after an exceptionally long church service, he made a paper boat and threw it at the preacher—his father. Years later, he confided: "It still hurts me to sit down when I think of it."

The Seagrave family came back to

the United States in 1909, for the sake
of twelve-year-old Gordon's schooling.
When he had caught up on subjects he
missed in Burma, he went to Denison
University in Ohio. There he worked
as a waiter to pay part of his expenses;
he got so good at his job that he could
carry food for eighteen people on one
tray.

From carrying the heavy trays, he
developed such strength in his arms and
shoulders that he made the pole-vaulting
team. But the fun of campus life never
once swayed him from his main goal.
That was to learn all he could about
medicine, so he could return to Burma
as a medical missionary.

Thus, after being graduated from
Denison, he enrolled in Johns Hopkins
University in Baltimore to study medicine. He found time to go out for pole-
vaulting there, too. One of his cher-
ished souvenirs was a newspaper clip-
ping: "POLE VAULT—SEAGRAVE, JOHNS
HOPKINS, FIRST. NO OTHERS RAN." But he
still kept his mind set on Burma.

During one summer he worked at a
camp in Wisconsin, which turned out to
be a most rewarding experience. He met
a girl on the camp staff who was fascinated by his plans for the future and
wanted nothing more than to share them.
Two years later, they were married.

By then, the young husband was finishing his medical training, but he still
needed the day-to-day familiarity with
treating patients that only a stint at a
busy hospital could provide. In his case,
any extra scientific background he could
pick up would be exceptionally valuable,
because he was bound for a part of the
world where there would be no oppor-

*Young Gordon Seagrave was determined to
be a medical missionary in Burma.*

tunities to consult learned specialists. At
the Baltimore hospital where he spent a
year, he also had the foresight to collect
a wastebasket full of discarded surgical
instruments.

With these and his wife and newborn
baby, Dr. Seagrave sailed for Burma in
1922. Arriving in Rangoon, he once
more came across that fascinating tale-
teller, Dr. Harper. Soon to retire, the
older man offered young Dr. Seagrave
his hospital at Namkham, far to the
north in the British-controlled country.

It was not easy to get there. The Seagraves traveled by train as far as Manda-
lay, then up the Irrawaddy River by
steamer to Bhamo. Then they had to
take to native ponies, which could man-

age no more than twelve miles a day along jungle trails. No hardships fazed them, though, because they were so anxious to reach Namkham and their life's work.

A less courageous young couple would have despaired when they finally saw the "hospital" that was now theirs. Its walls were almost crumbling with rot, its floors so filthy and rotted that walking was almost impossible. The Seagraves wept at the dismal sight.

But the next morning Dr. Seagrave decided that even if Namkham was not what he had hoped, he would make it so. Then started the first phase in the career of the man whom Americans would come to celebrate by the simple title of "The Burma Surgeon." As for the Burmese among whom he lived and worked at healing for so many years, they came to love him as few Westerners have ever been revered in Asia.

Dr. Seagrave began winning the confidence of the villagers by learning their languages. Already he knew how to speak one tribal dialect, Karen, and he soon picked up enough in the other dialects to make himself understood.

Then he went visiting from village to village, calling upon the headman and announcing that he had free medicine for the sick. The fact that this kindly-seeming stranger could talk to them in their own languages made the people trust him, and soon patients came flocking. For some, his stock of pills provided help enough. But for others, surgical operations proved necessary.

The problems he faced in operating would have daunted many another man. His supply of surgical equipment was extremely limited, he had no proper operating room even after the hospital was repaired and at the beginning his sole assistant was his own wife. Furthermore, his surgical training in Baltimore had only taught him basic procedures; many times he found himself having to perform an operation that he had never tried before.

On such occasions, he opened one of the books he had brought along and studied the technique described, as if he were still back in school. But confident as his manner was when he approached his patient the next morning, he once confessed that he always felt dreadfully sick to his stomach whenever he started on one of these untried operations. Still, many of them came out successfully.

In this first period of his Burma service, Dr. Seagrave adopted a policy that was to have important results later. To remedy his shortage of trained help, he opened his own school for nurses. Dainty Burmese girls with hardly any background in book learning studied such complicated subjects as anatomy in this remarkable establishment.

Dr. Seagrave first had to solve the language problem. His student body comprised girls from more than a dozen different tribal backgrounds—and each knew only her own language. The girls spoke Karen or Shan, Maru or Atsi, and were familiar with only a few sentences of the Burmese language that the British-run government had been trying to foster.

So Dr. Seagrave had to provide lessons in language as well as in nursing practice. And he also had to keep in mind constantly the variety of traditions fos-

"Batter up!" Dr. Seagrave coaches a nurse in a favorite American sport.

tered by the different tribes. To the Kachin girls, he had to speak in a commanding tone; they liked loud and positive voices. But the Karen girls became positively ill if anybody shouted at them.

Somehow Dr. Seagrave managed to cope with all of the special problems confronting his school. He even found an appropriate nickname by which all of his students could address him: "Daddy."

And not only did he turn out several classes of competent nurses. He also taught them baseball, which they played every Friday afternoon. "You can tell a lot about a nurse by the way she plays baseball," he commented cheerfully.

Yet the school was only a small part of his accomplishment over the next twenty years. Within five years, he had a new cement hospital building, largely paid for with donations from church-goers in distant America. Then Dr. Seagrave was able to care for 5,000 bed patients a year, plus an additional 10,000 patients who received treatment without having to be

hospitalized. "We have had them walk fifteen days on foot to get here," Dr. Seagrave once noted.

But all this had to be abandoned when the Japanese attacked Pearl Harbor and several outposts of Western influence in Asia, in December 1941. Burma was among the Japanese targets.

No longer could Dr. Seagrave concentrate on curing peaceful villagers. Now he and his corps of dainty but surprisingly sturdy nurses had a new and urgent task. Burma suddenly was a battleground. The British wanted Dr. Gordon Seagrave, American though he was, to command their emergency medical service.

Rather than chance the loss of his American citizenship, he turned down a commission as a lieutenant colonel in the British Army; but he accepted the mission. After sending his wife and children home to the United States, he set about organizing front-line field hospitals to treat battle casualties. These hospitals treated both British soldiers and Chinese troops, who were fighting side by side to repel the Japanese invaders. Then when the United States sent Lieutenant General Joseph W. ("Vinegar Joe") Stilwell to Burma, the medical units went under American command. Dr. Seagrave became a major in the Medical Corps of the United States Army.

Tall and spare, with gold-rimmed glasses and thinning hair, Dr. Seagrave may not have looked like much of a soldier, but he proved he had the staying power that counted more. With the Japanese infantry advancing and Japanese planes swooping down to drop bombs day and night, hundreds of military and civilian casualties kept arriving at his main emergency hospital.

Working in the hot sun, sweat streaming down his face, Dr. Seagrave examined the worst of the wounded. Once for thirty-six hours he stood over a makeshift operating table, trying to put shattered bones together. The heat was so ferocious that after a time he took off his surgeon's gown, then his shirt and his undershirt. Soon Dr. Seagrave was operating clad only in a pair of bloody shorts.

Day after day, as Japanese bombs fell nearby, while nurses scrambled into ditches to escape being hit, Dr. Seagrave kept on, harassed not only by the Japanese but also by fatigue, heat and insects. With little food and less sleep, he carried on his healing work.

All the time, even on the worst days, he did his best to bolster the spirits of his nurses. Speaking of the modern little hospital at Namkham, he would tell them: "We'll be back for Christmas."

But the Allies' plight steadily worsened, and they were forced into a great retreat, taking the wounded with them. They could go in only one direction— up over the hills and then through the jungle to India. At first, the retreating Allies traveled by trucks and jeeps, but then the trails grew too steep and they had to go on by foot, taking only those supplies that could be carried on their backs.

Seen on a map, the distance they covered may seem comparatively short, but on the ground the going was horrible. Following narrow trails, they inched up high mountains and through dense jungle. Broken bamboo shoots pierced the worn shoes of the soldiers.

One evening Dr. Seagrave lay down on a blanket, trying to gain some re-

After the Japanese invaded Burma, Dr. Seagrave worked to save lives at the front.

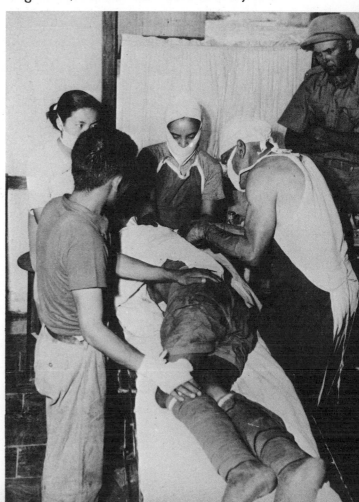

lief from the chilling malaria he had contracted.

"What's the matter, Seagrave, got fever?" General Stilwell asked.

"No, sir," Dr. Seagrave lied bravely. "I got wet and felt a little cold, so I was warming up."

"How are your feet?"

"Better, sir."

"You are lying."

"Yes, sir."

General Stilwell laughed. That made it a little easier. But there was nothing anyone could do except keep on, day after day, step after step. They went by raft up the Chindwin River, then up and down narrow mountain trails through the Naga Hills, famous for their head-hunters. Luckily, the savage tribesmen avoided the retreating army.

Startlingly enough, Dr. Seagrave's dainty Burmese nurses proved the best travelers—and morale raisers. Somehow their delicate feet did not weaken; they dashed into the jungle at mealtimes and returned with exotic native berries. They sang and they laughed. Many a dispirited soldier looking at them made up his mind that if these tiny nurses could take it, so could he.

Dr. Seagrave and his nurses, General Stilwell and the soldiers, all made it to the Assam Hills of India, to prepare to fight another day. General Stilwell vowed that he would return to Burma, and so did Dr. Seagrave.

But it took time. Christmas of 1942 passed and Dr. Seagrave was unable to keep his promise about going back to Namkham. Not till March of 1943 were the troops ready to begin the journey. General Stilwell led them out of India

on a new supply road constructed by Army engineers. At the border, they passed a new sign: "WELCOME TO BURMA. THIS WAY TO TOKYO." And as they rolled onward, American Air Force planes dropped food and ammunition ahead of them.

Still the road back was slow, slower even than the retreat. They had to stop and build bases; they had to stop and fight detachments of Japanese. They advanced step by step, back through the Naga Hills, over the mountains and through the jungles. And right behind the fighting men were Dr. Seagrave and his nurses, with their mobile hospital.

It took almost a year for the Allied troops to reach Myitkyina, a key city of Kachin State in Northern Burma. Once more Christmas passed and Dr. Seagrave had not kept his promise. Not till October of 1944 could the Allies mount a big drive to recapture the Namkham area.

On the day before Christmas of 1944, Dr. Seagrave gathered the nurses whose homes were in Namkham. He took them to a mountain lookout to show them the valley they loved, some fifteen miles away. But stubborn Japanese resistance kept the fighting going two more weeks. In the middle of January of 1945, Dr. Seagrave and his nurses finally came home again.

Together they climbed past a sign reading: "HEADQUARTERS, NAMKHAM GARRISON, IMPERIAL JAPANESE ARMY." They found bomb craters everywhere; and the hospital was severely damaged. But from out of the hills, from near and far, Burmese friends of Dr. Seagrave were arriving. They carried shovels and baskets;

A nurse dances for joy on the return to Namkham. Dr. Seagrave watches at right.

they were ready to work at whatever had to be done in order to restore the hospital as soon as possible. They would not accept the slightest payment for their work.

Despite the fact that he had just missed Christmas, Dr. Seagrave said he would have his party anyway. He invited everybody—natives, nurses, generals, soldiers. He expected about 300 guests, but more than 1,500 appeared. It was a wonderful personal tribute to the 47-year-old Burma Surgeon.

By now his face was deeply lined, and his knees felt wobbly if he tried to stand up too long. But even when the war ended and he could have retired to comfort and honor in the United States, Dr. Seagrave preferred to stay on in Burma. Like the European Dr. Albert Schweitzer and the American Dr. Tom Dooley, who brought their healing arts to other distant lands, he would not consider abandoning his work.

From the American Medical Center for Burma and from many strangers who read his book, *Burma Surgeon,* Dr. Seagrave received financial support to rebuild and expand his hospital. After Burma gained its independence in 1948, he remained a valued medical leader there.

But in the turbulent political struggles following independence, Dr. Seagrave was caught up in a factional dispute. Because of his policy of helping any Burmese who needed medical attention, he was arrested on a charge of treason in 1950; specifically, his crime was treating several rebellious tribesmen.

Convicted and sentenced to six years in prison, he refused to turn bitter toward the Burmese; philosophically, he considered the incident as not really

Dr. Seagrave among his patients.

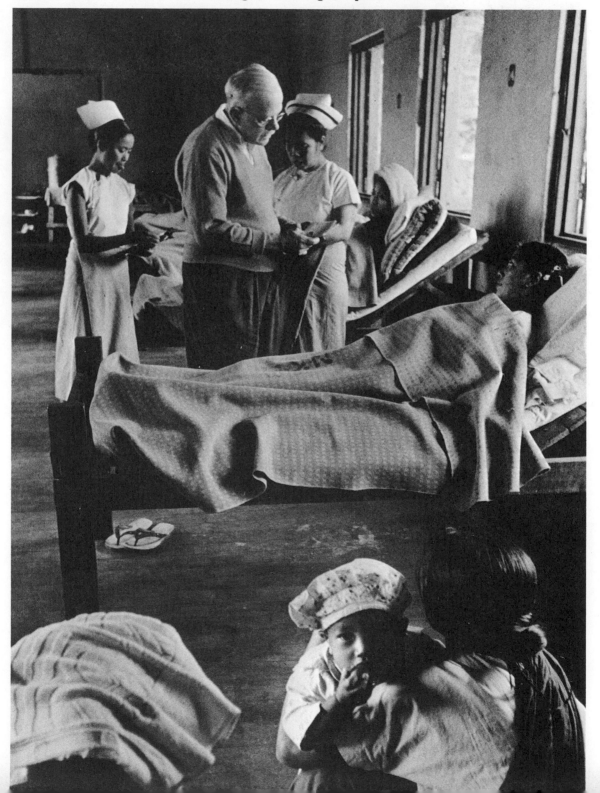

important. Indeed, he was treated very kindly for a prisoner, being housed in the warden's own home in Rangoon and given a personal servant. His biggest problem was finding a way to spend his time.

After sixteen months of prison, even the officials who had accused him realized the absurdity of their action. Completely cleared of all charges, Dr. Seagrave started back to the hospital at Namkham.

As he drove up the familiar road, men, women and children crowded around him, shouting, cheering, weeping. "The 'Old Man' is back!" they cried. And he was back to stay. During the next several years, he kept expanding his hospital, treating more patients, training more nurses. Having survived disease, poverty and war in his long effort to help the people of Burma, Dr. Seagrave died in his own hospital in 1965 at the age of sixty-eight.

Not long before his death, he had spoken his inner feelings to an interviewer. "If I haven't done my country as much good as I have done Burma, then I have wasted my life," he said. But that he had truly served the United States—by giving the whole world the inspiring picture of a selfless American —could not be doubted.

After his death the Burmese Government took over Dr. Seagrave's hospital in Namkham. His many friends in the United States paid him the tribute he would have appreciated most: They established the Seagrave Memorial Hospital in the remote village of Kaejong in South Korea, another far-off Asian land.

MARGARET BOURKE-WHITE
Photographer of Valor

Only a few months after the United States entered World War II, an odd scene was enacted in Washington. Solemn-faced Army officers stood considering bolts of green and gray cloth. An assortment of buttons was passed from hand to hand. The baffling question at issue: What should the well-dressed woman war correspondent or photographer wear overseas?

Watching all this, Margaret Bourke-White was amused—and pleased. Slender and feminine as she looked, with her short, curly brown hair and blue eyes, Miss Bourke-White was already well accustomed to leading the way for other women into areas previously dared only by men. Even as a girl she had been unusual.

It seemed to her that much of the credit for whatever she accomplished belonged to her parents. Born on June 14, 1906, in New York City and named Margaret Bourke White, she grew up in the small New Jersey town of Bound Brook. She went through a period when she was terrified of the dark; with games instead of lectures, her mother gently helped her conquer this fear completely. But it was her father, an engineer, who all but erased fear from her vocabulary. He did it with snakes.

Taking her on nature walks, he told her all about snakes and their habits, till she was so fascinated she quite forgot to be afraid of them. Together Mr. White and his daughter built wire cages to house a growing collection of snakes. Even before she finished high school, Margaret knew so much about snakes that she took it for granted she would be a herpetologist, as a snake expert is known among scientists.

With such an unusual ambition, obviously she stood more than slightly apart from other girls her age. If Margaret seemed peculiar to her classmates, that made no difference to her mother. Mrs. White had strict ideas about raising children and did not want her daughter to be frivolous. Margaret had to wear cotton stockings when the other girls wore silk; she could go to the movies only once in a great while.

If Margaret felt more than slightly disappointed because boys never asked her to dances, she still kept happy most of the time at her particular hobby. When she won a school-wide writing contest, with the prize being three books of her own selection, she chose books on frogs, moths and snakes.

By the year she went off to college, photography had begun to interest her, too, and she signed up for a photography course in her first term. But reptiles were still her main concern until she transferred to the University of Michigan the next year and met a young man who was studying engineering. She spent the next several months thoroughly enjoying being escorted to dances by this young man. At the age of nineteen, she married him.

Too inexperienced to have known she was not ready for the responsibility of marriage, she learned her mistake quickly and was soon divorced. She also had to face a serious financial problem. She still wanted to finish college and specialize in herpetology, but the death of her father left her without the money she would need.

She had chosen to continue her studies at Cornell in upper New York State, not only because it offered good science training, but also because of its scenery. Having read about the picturesque waterfalls on the campus, she had a yearning to see them.

On arriving at Cornell, she found that the waitress job she had hoped for was already taken. There were no jobs left in the library, either. In desperation she took out her camera; it struck her that other students might be fascinated by the falls. She snapped picture after picture, not only of the falls but of all sorts of scenic vistas around the campus. She concentrated, too, on trying to capture the charm of various ivy-covered campus buildings.

Then, shortly before Christmas, she set up a sales stand outside a dining hall —and her photographs soon sold out. The alumni magazine printed a series of her pictures, and letters began to arrive, filled with praise for her artistry. Several letters pointed out that few photographers had the special ability to take interesting pictures of buildings, and that the field of architectural photography was wide open.

Here was an idea that caused Margaret to think hard, because as her graduation day approached she had a chance to work for the Museum of Natural History in New York. This would be the first step toward a career in herpetology.

Torn between the two possibilities, she decided to go to New York and show a portfolio of her pictures to a leading architect. If he thought they were not good enough, she would take the museum job.

The architect's verdict was quick and conclusive. With those pictures to her credit, he told her, she could walk into any architecture office in the country and get photography assignments. From that day onward, snakes definitely took second place.

Upon graduation, Margaret Bourke White moved to Cleveland, where she had lived briefly during her marriage and which she now considered home. She also decided to add a hyphen between her middle name and her last name. She felt that Bourke-White had an impressive look and sound for a woman embarking on a career like hers. She was still only twenty-one when she opened the Bourke-White Studios in 1927.

Before that day in 1942 when she turned up to be measured for the first female war correspondent's uniform, she had almost fifteen years to demon-

One of many daring assignments—photographing New York City from the top of the Chrysler Building, 1000 feet above the ground.

strate her extraordinary talent—and determination.

When she started, photographic lenses were far less sophisticated than they would be in later decades, lighting was poor, the photographic paper in common use left much to be desired. Working tirelessly to find better tools, as well as to improve her own skills, Margaret Bourke-White earned a reputation as one of America's best photographers.

She photographed dams and factories, stockyards and steel mills, bridges and skyscrapers. Her pictures were so good that she was asked to work for a new magazine that planned to emphasize photography; a Margaret Bourke-White photograph of Fort Peck Dam in Mon-

tana was on the cover of the first issue of *Life* in 1936.

When Germany attacked Russia in 1941, she happened to be in Moscow on an assignment. That was her first taste of war, and the pictures she took of Moscow under fire brought her first taste of fame. The woman photographer with the quick smile and the determined chin became a heroine in her own right. By now she was married again, to the writer Erskine Caldwell, yet she knew what she wanted to do after Pearl Harbor. It never occurred to her that she might be kept from photographing the war in Europe because she was a woman. Without too much difficulty, she convinced her editors to send her on that dangerous mission.

69

Her husband did not object because he and she decided their careers required their going separate ways; they divorced but remained friendly.

But she did have to convince the Army. Without formal approval from military authorities, no civilian could enter a war zone. Maggie, as the men she worked with called her, came back from Washington not only with the proper papers in her purse, but also with a brand-new uniform. Designed on the same basic pattern as the standard officers' garb, it had a skirt; slacks were provided for field wear.

In England, Maggie took pictures of Winston Churchill and of gaunt-faced airmen stepping down from their planes, returning from bombing missions deep in Germany. But she had a little difficulty in getting permission to go along on a raid.

When the invasion of North Africa was planned, she hoped to be able to ride with a bomber crew at last. But once more she was turned down by the top brass, on the grounds that the assignment would be too risky for a woman. Instead, she was given permission to ride on a troopship that would be part of a protected convoy.

The night before the ship was due to arrive off North Africa, a torpedo struck it. Miss Bourke-White grabbed her camera and ran for the deck. Her mouth was dry. With some surprise, she thought: "This must be fear."

There were 6,000 troops, including a small group of nurses, aboard the ship. Swiftly, but with some inevitable confusion, lifeboats were lowered. Still holding her camera, Maggie found herself

Maggie drinking hot Ovaltine aboard the destroyer that rescued her at sea.

sitting in a crowded small boat. A soldier swam up. "Hi, taxi!" he called. A nurse wearing a lifejacket paddled along as if she were enjoying herself and called: "Which way to North Africa?" To keep spirits up, the men and women in the lifeboat sang: "You are my sunshine, my only sunshine."

After sunrise, she took pictures of her boatmates and helped bail out the leaky little boat with a helmet. By midafternoon, she had the pleasure of photographing her fellow survivors as they waved excitedly at the friendly plane that had spotted them. Before nightfall, she was safely aboard a rescue destroyer.

Although she would admit now that she knew what fear was, Miss Bourke-White did not propose to change her plans. She still thought the best way to tell the story of the war in the air was to photograph an actual bombing run. She had almost given up hoping she might

70

get the opportunity when she bumped into an old friend, General Jimmy Doolittle, in North Africa.

"Maggie, do you still want to go on a bombing mission?" he asked her.

"Oh, you know I do!" she told him. "I had given up asking, because I didn't want to make a nuisance of myself all the time."

"Well, you've been torpedoed," he said. "You might as well go through everything." And via field telephone he relayed his permission for her to accompany a combat flight.

On January 22, 1943, huddled in a thick flying suit, Maggie Bourke-White took off in a B-17 bound for Tunis, then held by the Germans. Two other planes in the same group were shot down, and her own plane was hit twice by antiaircraft fire. But the pilot managed to bring it back safely, and the pictures taken en route were printed under the headline: "LIFE'S BOURKE-WHITE GOES BOMBING." But the photographer was flattered even more when a picture of herself, swathed in a leather flying suit and standing beside the parked plane, her camera in hand, became popular as a morale-boosting pin-up at air bases.

Her next assignment was with ground forces in Italy. Stalled just below the mountain town of Monte Cassino, the American infantry was under fierce fire

Her camera always in hand, Maggie takes cover behind sandbags at the Italian front.

by German cannon. With four different cameras to capture a variety of views, Maggie stood her ground, loading and firing on her own, till the whoosh of a shell coming right at her forced her to scramble for shelter in a ditch.

In the nurses' tent after her pictures were taken, she carefully put her cameras under a table for safety. Then came another blast, and she shoved the cameras aside so she could get under the table herself.

After this, most civilians would have had enough of the war, but Miss Bourke-White was not ready to give up. After a brief rest in the United States, she returned to Italy and traveled with the Allied troops as they fought their way north of Rome. Enduring every hardship the infantry suffered, she sometimes had the extra aggravation of finding that her pictures, taken at such risk to life and limb, had somehow been lost on their way back to be printed. Yet no matter how discouraged, she refused to quit.

As the war neared its end, she accompanied General George B. Patton's Third Army, advancing ever deeper into Germany. She was with them when they reached the infamous death camp of Buchenwald, where tens of thousands of Nazi victims had been murdered. She saw and photographed the horrifying piles of naked, lifeless bodies.

"People often ask me how it is possible to photograph such atrocities," she wrote later. "I have to work with a veil over my mind. In photographing the murder camps, the protective veil was so tightly drawn that I hardly knew what I had taken until I saw prints of my own photographs. It was as though I was seeing these horrors for the first time . . ."

Yet she could never shirk such an assignment, she explained, for to do so would be to shirk the obligation she had willingly assumed when she became a war correspondent. It was her duty, she felt, to pass on to others—via her camera—the facts of war, terrible though they were.

When the war ended, Miss Bourke-White went next to India, then on the eve of independence. She photographed Mahatma Gandhi many times, including the day before he was assassinated, and she photographed his funeral.

Returning to the United States then, she settled in a house on a rocky Connecticut hill and wrote a book about her experiences. Next came an assignment to South Africa, and then to cover another war—in Korea.

One day in Korea she noticed a dull ache in her left leg. Instead of disappearing the pain got worse, till she had difficulty walking. Back in the United States, she discovered that the trouble was Parkinson's disease, a frightening ailment which could cause very serious crippling. The medical verdict staggered Miss Bourke-White.

Through two wars and countless other dangerous adventures, she had always thought of herself as "Maggie the Indestructible." Now she faced an enemy which could soon make her helpless, could turn her every muscle rigid, preventing any movement at all. Already she could hardly walk.

But having learned to ignore fear, Miss Bourke-White refused to give in now. Thus started the most courageous struggle of her life—a battle not merely on her own behalf, but for the benefit of uncounted thousands also suffering from the same disease.

To give them hope that help was possible, she allowed the story of her own determined effort to be told in the magazine with which she had been so closely identified. She would have preferred privacy; she wanted no headlines now, or sympathy. But she was willing to break through the secrecy usually surrounding cases of the disease because she felt that the secrecy itself was the worst evil.

Most people finding themselves victims of the disease refused to admit the fact, she wrote. And yet their situation was not as hopeless as they might think. Then she described her own unremitting fight to arrest the symptoms, by dogged exercising and by submitting to operations that might also help other victims.

When a second operation brought still further improvement, she described how she had been able to take a jumping rope out of her pocketbook and give a little demonstration.

"Through the sphere of the moving rope, I could hear the surprised exclamations of my delighted doctors," she reported. "This gave me special pleasure, as there was a time, not so far back, when mastery of a jumping rope seemed more impossible of attainment than a trip to the moon."

Realistically accepting the fact that her cure could never be complete enough for her to get to the moon—an assignment her editors had promised her some years earlier—Miss Bourke-White settled down to quiet retirement at her Connecticut home.

But although she was removed now

"Maggie the Indestructible" at home, exercising her hands by crumpling paper.

from the great events which she was used to photographing, "Maggie the Indestructible" was more of a heroine than ever. For her bravery in the face of a cruel personal enemy, she had earned still higher honor and warmer praise than her camera had already helped her to win.

ROBERT GODDARD
Father of Rocketry

A frail boy of seventeen climbed the cherry tree in back of the barn near his home on the outskirts of Worcester, Massachusetts, on the afternoon of October 19, 1899. Armed with a saw and a hatchet, he started to trim dead branches. But it was a beautiful fall afternoon, and he stopped to look at the colorful leaves on the nearby trees. He began to daydream.

How wonderful it would be to leave the earth's surface and travel into space, possibly even to Mars! How could he make a machine that could travel into the sky? He sat considering the question, and a thought came to him. "It seemed to me then that a weight, whirling around a horizontal shaft and moving more rapidly above than below, could furnish lift by virtue of the greater centrifugal force at the top of the path," he recalled later.

Obviously Robert Hutchings Goddard was no ordinary daydreaming boy. Born in Worcester on October 5, 1882, he had been a sickly child, continually coming down with colds. Encouraged by his father, he had always shown an interest in science and experiments. After he was taken out of school because of bad health, he began a program of self-education in the sciences.

He tried to make diamonds at home by heating graphite, but an explosion ended that experiment. He pounded a bar of aluminum into a round shape, installed a valve and then tried to fill it with hydrogen. But he sadly noted in his diary: "Aluminum balloon will not go up. Tried to put gas into it, but could not. Aluminum is too heavy. Failure crowns enterprise."

Despite all of his early experimenting, though, it was not till Robbie Goddard was seventeen that he finally settled on his life's work. When he climbed down from that cherry tree, he knew his goal for the rest of his days would be to discover a way to fly into space. "Life now had a purpose for me," he said later.

Immediately he set to work to manufacture wooden models of his spaceship. He used whirling lead weights to furnish power for lifting his device off the ground. But somehow the machine didn't work. He began to pay more attention to the theory of physics, especially Newton's third law: for every action, there is an equal and opposite reaction. He realized that if he was ever going to find a way to get into space, he would have to know more about mathematics and physics.

Despite his illness, he returned to high

Seventeen-year-old Robert and his mother at home in Worcester.

school and began to study seriously. In his first year there, in December 1901, he wrote an article on space navigation and sent it to *Popular Science Monthly*. It was rejected. Still he persevered in building models of projected space vehicles, none of which worked. One day, as he neared the end of his high-school course, he decided that he would have to start all over again. He gathered all his models and all his notes and burned them in a little wooden stove in the dining room.

The long string of failures did not stop Robbie. He enrolled in 1904 at the Worcester Polytechnic Institute to study engineering and physics, buying himself some green-covered notebooks in which he systematically recorded all his ideas. For the next few years, almost all of these notes were about rockets and rocket propulsion.

The main problem with rockets, all his studies at Worcester and later at Clark University indicated to him, was propulsion. How could you get sufficient power to lift a rocket off the ground without blowing it up? He had already come to the conclusion that bags of gas, used in balloons, and moving propellers, used in airplanes, could never lift objects to great heights. What then?

His first tests were with gunpowder; he was perhaps inspired by Jules Verne, whose fictional voyagers from the earth to the moon were shot from a cannon. But Goddard's tests failed. Perhaps a series of cannon, firing in sequence with each falling off as it completed its job, would work. But this too seemed hopelessly complicated.

In 1909 Goddard wrote in his notebooks: "Try, if possible, for an arrangement of H & O explosive jets with compressed gas in small tanks which are subsequently shut off . . ." This was the first suggestion for a liquid-fueled rocket using hydrogen as the fuel and supplying sufficient oxygen to burn it efficiently. No one had ever before tried this.

Two years later Goddard completed his studies at Clark University and received a Ph.D. degree. He taught for a while at Clark and then did research on a fellowship at Princeton. In 1913, he returned home to Worcester with a severe cough. The doctors diagnosed it as tuberculosis and gave him two weeks to live.

But Goddard fooled them. He was stronger than they thought and he had a mission to complete. He opened the windows wide, against the doctor's instructions, and breathed deeply. His health began to improve. And, while lying in bed, he concentrated on rocket problems.

He worked out solutions in his head so well that he was able to make drawings of rockets with precise details of the parts that would be needed. He applied for and received two patents for rockets that had not yet been built or tested.

The first patent was essentially a practical proposal for a multistaged rocket, in which the secondary engine would not ignite until after the first had finished firing. It was a refinement of his earlier idea of using cannon shots in sequence. The second patent provided for a combustion chamber into which a liquid fuel and liquid oxygen would be fed for continuous burning and propulsion. The drawings that accompanied the patent applications look remarkably similar to drawings of modern rockets. As a matter of fact, the patents are basic to our rocket and space programs today.

When Goddard recovered, he was skinny and frail and almost bald. He returned to his teaching at Clark—and to his experiments. But his salary of $1,000 a year was scarcely enough to support himself and his experiments too. He decided to apply to the Smithsonian Institution in Washington for a research grant.

His application was called simply "A Method of Reaching Extreme Altitudes." In summary, what he said was that he could build a rocket motor more efficient than any existing engine, which could lift a small load perhaps as high as thirty-five miles.

In Washington, where scientists were extremely interested in probing the upper atmosphere so that they could make better weather predictions, his proposals were received enthusiastically. He was granted $5,000 to continue his experiments.

When the United States entered the First World War shortly afterward, Goddard proposed that his rockets be used for military purposes. Rockets had been used in warfare before, of course. The Chinese had fired rockets some 700 years earlier; the British used them against Napoleon and against the Americans in the War of 1812. But these early rockets were complex and more spectacular than deadly. What Goddard did was to

A page from Goddard's notebook of 1912. Especially prophetic was the "further work" section, in which he proposed to send a camera to the moon.

Goddard demonstrating his rocket weapon during World War I.

make his rocket simple and effective. He turned his rocket launcher sideways; instead of going up, the rocket—now the shell—would go horizontally and thus could be aimed at an enemy target. Moreover, the rocket principle would eliminate the problem of recoil, which heretofore had made it impossible for a soldier to carry too powerful a weapon.

In November 1918 Goddard was ready for a practical demonstration. One of his aides held the rocket launcher in his hands. Without any kickback, or recoil, the rockets blasted through several bags of sand. It was an impressive demonstration, and the Army officers indicated that they would put the rocket into production. But the war ended a few days later and the demonstration was forgotten. (It wasn't until World War II broke out, more than twenty years later, that Goddard's invention was taken off the shelf and developed into the famous bazooka rocket that destroyed or disabled many enemy tanks.)

For Goddard, at the end of the First World War, it was back to college and more experiments. In 1920 he became famous and an object of ridicule, not because of his experiments, but because of a scientific report.

In that year, the Smithsonian Institution published his paper on ways to reach high altitudes. In a press release the Institution noted one of Goddard's speculations: the possibility of sending a rocket to the moon and, upon landing, of igniting a magnesium flare that could be seen from the earth.

Then, as now, the possibility of reaching the moon excited the public and the press. Headlines all over the country trumpeted his story. Goddard became known as the inventor of the moon rocket. His proposal had in fact been much more modest; his aim was merely to develop a rocket that could go several miles up into the air. But he did not budge from the implications: the same principle that would lift a rocket one mile into the air would carry it to the moon. All that was needed was sufficient money for research and development.

Many scoffed at Goddard as impractical; they called him "Moony" Goddard or "Moon Mad" Goddard. But his ideas aroused serious interest abroad, especially in Germany. Rocket enthusiasts in that country wrote to him for more information, and he sent copies of his Smithsonian paper to them.

Doggedly, he went back to his research. He was truly a "lone wolf" operator, working with a few assistants in his own laboratory in Worcester. Day by day, his diaries recorded experiments. But his nozzles split, the chambers cracked, the pumps jammed. A less determined man might have given up, but Goddard was patient—and confident. He was positive his rocket would work.

78

The proud inventor with the first liquid-fuel rocket, just before its test flight on March 16, 1926.

He interrupted his work in 1924 to marry Esther Kisk, whom he had met while she was a secretary at the college and who had agreed to type his papers after school hours. Now he had not only a wife but also a trusted assistant, who quickly found out that rockets were never far from his thoughts. On their honeymoon she discovered him working on a manuscript. He was revising Verne's *From the Earth to the Moon* to bring it up to date.

Two years later, after hundreds of experiments, Goddard was ready for his first major test outdoors. It was March 16, 1926, a clear, cold day with snow on the ground, when he and his assistants went out to his test site, the Ward farm in nearby Auburn, Massachusetts. The farm was owned by a distant relative, his Aunt Effie Ward.

The rocket being tested was about ten feet long, with an engine to give it power, an exhaust nozzle and some fins to stabilize it in flight. It sat in a vertical position inside a homemade launching frame made of pipes. There was no remote-control system to ignite the fuel; one of the men set off the combustion with an alcohol stove. Behind a sheet-iron barricade Goddard waited, watching anxiously. Mrs. Goddard started to take moving pictures (which unfortunately did not turn out).

The rocket did not rise at first, but flames did come out, indicating a successful combustion. Then after what seemed an agonizingly long time, the rocket

Robert Goddard with two of his supporters, Harry Guggenheim (left) and Charles Lindbergh (right).

finally rose until it cleared the pipe frame and climbed into the sky. It curved to the left and crashed into the ground. It had risen 41 feet in two and a half seconds and it had traveled 184 feet.

That was the first successful flight in the history of modern rocketry. To Goddard, the flight was a vindication of his cherry-tree dream. He compared it to the first small flight of the Wright brothers' airplane, unimpressive if measured only in terms of the distance traveled, but a milestone of design and a promise for the future.

For three years Goddard worked patiently with nozzles, pumps, valves and combustion chambers, making his own designs in a field in which no other American was working, and manufacturing the parts that no company had ever dreamed of. It wasn't until July 17, 1929, that he was ready for another major test.

His new model, eleven and a half feet long, twenty-six inches wide and thirty-five pounds in weight, was transported to Aunt Effie's farm. Once more the rocket was launched by the primitive means of the alcohol stove. With flames shooting out from under and with a noisy roar, the rocket climbed to about 80 feet before it crashed to the earth. The experimenters were elated.

But then off in the distance they heard sirens shrieking and coming closer. A police car and two ambulances roared up. Where's the plane crash? the police asked. Neighbors who had heard the noise had reported an explosion.

Goddard explained that there was no crash. He was merely conducting some rocket experiments.

Reporters, remembering that Goddard was the "moon rocket" man, wrote that he had attempted a flight to the moon and had failed. Once again, Goddard was held up to ridicule because "sensible" people knew that a flight to the moon was impossible. More important, the fire marshal ordered him to conduct his experiments elsewhere, where they would not endanger people.

Goddard went back to his laboratory discouraged, not because of the experiment but because people did not understand what he was trying to do. A telephone call shortly afterward changed the situation.

The caller was Charles A. Lindbergh, the hero of the solo transatlantic airplane flight. He had read about Goddard's experiments in *The New York Times* and wanted to know more. He visited the laboratories and talked with Goddard.

"What would help you most in carrying out your experiments?" Lindbergh asked.

Goddard replied that he wanted to be free of his classroom work and that he needed a place to experiment without worry about the neighbors.

Out of this conversation came a grant of $50,000 for two years work and the promise of $50,000 more later from a special fund provided by Daniel Guggenheim. At last Goddard would be free to conduct his experiments without distraction.

He looked around the country until he found the ideal place for his experiments, a location with good clear weather the year round and few people. He chose Roswell, New Mexico.

In 1930, Goddard and his wife moved there. At the center of his test range in the wide-open country was a machine shop. Nearby was a static test frame, where the rocket could be tested without going into the air. The location was superb.

Before he could make a bigger and better rocket, Goddard faced three major technical jobs: building a better lightweight engine; perfecting a guidance system to keep the rocket erect in flight; and designing miniature pumps to feed the liquid fuels and oxygen into the combustion chamber.

Step by step he ran his tests, replacing defective parts, designing new equipment, manufacturing parts when needed. A careful, cautious man about equipment, Goddard made sure he patented all his devices.

His rockets showed steady improvement, but these were years of alternate progress and discouragement. It was painstaking work, but he was encouraged by the interest of Lindbergh and the financial support of the Daniel and Florence Guggenheim Foundation.

One of his rockets went 2,000 feet into the air, but the next one rose only 200 feet. Some of the test rockets never left the ground. By 1935, though, Goddard had sent one 7,000 feet up—more than a mile high—the highest rocket flight ever recorded up to that point.

Despite the slow pace of the work, Goddard himself was not discouraged. He knew that his principles were sound and that, with time, work and money, the rockets would be successful.

In 1938 a distant hurricane, far from New Mexico, did shake him a bit. The hurricane swept over New England, knocking down houses and trees. A message from Worcester informed him that the old cherry tree, the one he had climbed back in 1899, had been among the victims of the storm. On October 19, 1939, the fortieth anniversary of the day he climbed the tree, he wrote in one of his notebooks: "Cherry tree down. Have to carry on alone."

The Second World War had already started in Europe and once more Goddard volunteered himself and his work to the military. Once again, however, the military services were not overly enthusiastic, mainly because the military has always been reluctant to accept new ideas.

The Navy did accept his offer finally. Goddard and his staff later went to work at the research laboratories at Annapolis, Maryland. Their job was to perfect jet-assisted takeoffs (called JATO) for Navy planes. No one in the United States, apparently, was interested in the real potential of rockets in warfare.

It was a shock to many in the United States, but not to Goddard, when the Germans, who had always been interested in rocketry, suddenly attacked England with revolutionary rocket weapons of extraordinary power. London was mercilessly bombed with V-1 rockets and then the more powerful V-2s, launched from sites in Europe with a speed that made it impossible to knock them down.

Luckily for the Allies, they had the air power to pulverize the launch sites before their armies conquered the Nazis on the ground. When the war ended and the American experts entered the German rocket center at Peenemunde,

As Goddard's work progressed, his rockets went farther and farther into space.

they began to ask technical questions. The Germans were baffled.

"Why don't you ask your own Dr. Goddard?" one of them replied. The Germans knew, even if the American military leaders did not, that Robert Goddard had developed the concept of modern rocketry. The Germans had not only read his published reports; they had put his ideas to work.

Shortly afterward, one of the German rockets was brought back to the United States. Goddard and one of his aides inspected it.

"It looks like ours," the aide commented.

"Yes," Goddard replied, a little sadly, "it seems so."

At last the world had awakened to the reality of long-range rockets in war, and it was soon to recognize their potential for the exploration of space, just as Goddard had predicted. But it was too late for Goddard himself. He died on August 10, 1945, at the age of sixty-three, after an operation for throat cancer. It was only after his death that his country acknowledged his genius and his courage in carrying on in the face of resistance.

In 1960 the National Aeronautics and Space Administration and the military forces agreed to pay a million dollars for infringing on Goddard's patents in the space program. Government lawyers acknowledged that the Army, the Navy, the Air Force and the space agency had used his ideas without permission or payment in their missile and rocket programs. Most of the money went to the Daniel and Florence Guggenheim Foundation to repay the amounts it had advanced to Goddard for his experiments. In that same year, fifteen years after his death, Goddard was awarded the Langley Medal for achievements in aeronautics.

Then in 1961, on March 16, exactly thirty-five years after the pioneer rocket flight in Aunt Effie's meadow, NASA dedicated its center for space research in Greenbelt, Maryland, just outside Washington. It is the Goddard Space Flight Center.

And this year, and every year from now on, under terms of a law passed by Congress and signed by President Lyndon B. Johnson, Americans will mark March 16 as a day to be set aside in memory of Robert Hutchings Goddard, the American hero of science who set the world on the path to the moon and the stars.

FRANKLIN D. ROOSEVELT
Nothing to Fear but Fear Itself

He seemed serious and bookish as a boy —some of the time. That was when he pored over his stamp collection, or studied up on birds and naval battles, both of which fascinated him.

But he also loved to swim and sail and hunt and ride on horseback. He had his own pony, his own hunting dog, his own sailboat. It was no ordinary childhood that Franklin Delano Roosevelt enjoyed.

As a result, he was an unusual sort of child. He knew what it was like to stay in the best hotels in London and Paris before he knew many children of his own age. He had such good manners that he charmed adults easily, most especially his mother. When her voice took on its strict tone, he still could find a way to make her smile. One evening, for instance, while she was reading aloud to him and he was puttering on the floor with his stamps, she noticed he was paying her no attention at all.

"Franklin!" she said sharply. "I don't think there is any point in my reading to you any more. You don't hear me anyway."

Her son looked up with a glint of mischief in his eyes. "Why, Mama, I would be ashamed of myself if I couldn't do at least two things at once," he said.

His quick wit was rewarded as his mother smiled.

But besides this great gift of sensing how to please almost everybody, Franklin Roosevelt started life with many other advantages. He was tall and imposingly handsome; and from spending so many hours outdoors, he radiated an air of glowing good health.

By birth, he belonged to one of the most favored of families. Roosevelts had been living in New York ever since the earliest Dutch days in the seventeenth century; and being shrewd merchants, the first arrivals had prospered. Some of their descendants had been equally shrewd in business investments. Franklin's father, James Roosevelt, belonged to the branch of the family that had been settled comfortably for several generations on an estate overlooking the Hudson River near the hamlet of Hyde Park. Here Franklin had been born on January 30, 1882.

His mother had come from a similar background. Miss Sara Delano was a handsome, well-educated and wealthy young woman when she married James Roosevelt. He was a widower of fifty-two with one son already out in the world on his own. But the fact that Mr.

Young Franklin with his mother.

Roosevelt was twenty-six years older struck Miss Delano as no obstacle, and she was sufficiently strong-minded to overcome the disapproval voiced by her own family.

The age difference had a great effect on young Franklin. His father did take him sledding and sailing, and these were happy moments. Yet the declining state of Mr. Roosevelt's health gradually cut off such father-and-son companionship; after long months of invalidism, James Roosevelt died when Franklin was eighteen.

The loss of his father was the one real misfortune Franklin Roosevelt had to face in his growing-up years.

However, Franklin had always had one problem: he was the only child of an extraordinarily strong-willed mother. Sara Delano Roosevelt tried to plan his every day to the smallest detail. When she was past eighty, and her son was the President of the United States, he once remarked a little peevishly that he had never in his whole life gone out of doors without his mother calling after him: "Franklin! Are you sure you're dressed warmly enough?"

But long before FDR moved into the White House, he had learned how to deal with his mother. He loved her dearly, but he did not want her to make decisions for him. On little things, he could get his way by teasing her and making her laugh. On bigger questions, he found out quite early that power was the answer—will power. He had a good deal of practice even as a boy in strengthening his own will. It had acquired sufficient force to challenge hers by the time he was a senior at Harvard.

Mrs. Roosevelt had regretfully decided some years earlier, when Franklin was fourteen, that the time had come when he had to go away to school. Until then, he had done his lessons with private tutors, at Hyde Park or wherever the family traveled.

Franklin had a comparatively easy time at Groton, the highly regarded boarding school in Massachusetts to which he was sent. Although unaccustomed to boys his own age, he managed to get along. "He has been a thoroughly faithful scholar & a most satisfactory member of this school," his final report said.

At Harvard, he had gone even further in the direction of winning friends and influencing college activities. Competent if not outstanding in his studies, he had thrown himself eagerly into campus politics; he was unquestionably one of the most popular men at the college then. His enthusiasm over this sort of politicking struck Sara Delano Roosevelt as not quite gentlemanly. But her dismay over his office seeking was nothing in comparison with her upset when he announced in December of his senior year, during a quick visit to Hyde Park, that he planned to get married immediately after graduating.

It was not that she objected to his choice. Franklin's intended wife was entirely suitable from her own point of view, if any wife were needed. But Mrs. Roosevelt already had formed a clear picture of how she herself and Franklin would be spending the next ten years or so. They would alternate travel with peaceful months at Hyde Park, and should Franklin's active mind require stimulation, a gentlemanly law practice might be the answer. Perhaps later on, much later, he might marry, but certainly not so soon.

Franklin listened patiently; he would never refuse to hear out any objection to what he wanted to do. And he was willing to compromise; he would not insist on having his own way without regard to the wishes of others. After graduation he went on a summer trip with his mother, he enrolled in law school and the following year he did marry, with his mother's grudging approval.

His bride was a tall, shy girl whom he had first met when she visited Hyde Park with her parents as a baby. He had given her a ride around the nursery on his back then. She was his fifth cousin, once removed, Miss Anna Eleanor Roosevelt.

She was also the niece of the man who

Franklin and Eleanor at Campobello the summer before their marriage.

in recent years had put the name of Roosevelt on front pages everywhere. President Theodore Roosevelt was her late father's brother. So her Uncle Ted left the White House on March 17, 1905, to review the St. Patrick's Day Parade in New York—and to give away the bride at the wedding of his two young relatives.

Thus Franklin and Eleanor Roosevelt started their married life in a hectic crush of Secret Service men guarding a United States President. It was a fitting beginning.

Beyond doubt, Franklin already had a private yen to run for office even as early as his marriage. Nothing else at Harvard had given him the same heady feeling that he got from maneuvering behind the scenes to win a nomination or an election. Issues and ideas interested him less; there lay his main weakness. But if he could charm voters into choosing him, no matter that his platform was a bit vague; he thought he could always find a good program after he was elected.

It was a big jump from Senior Day chairman to President of the United States, but the example of his cousin Theodore surely inspired him. Within five years after his marriage, Franklin Roosevelt embarked actively on a political career.

The first office he sought was that of New York state senator. All through the early autumn of 1910, he bumped along the back roads of the Hyde Park neighborhood in a flag-draped open car, shaking hands with farmers. He was running as a Democrat—mainly, it seemed, because his father had quietly differed from the rest of the family in preferring to vote Democratic. Although the Hudson Valley was traditionally and solidly Republican, 28-year-old Franklin Roosevelt exerted enough charm to win that November.

With vaguely "progressive" leanings, he fought the power of New York City's Democratic bosses while he was in Albany, and also campaigned on behalf of New Jersey's Woodrow Wilson, who had open and immediate Presidential ambitions. When Wilson won in 1912, he appointed the young New Yorker as his Assistant Secretary of the Navy.

Roosevelt had always loved the sea and was an expert sailor as a result of years of summer yachting expeditions from the family's vacation house on Campobello Island, in Canada off the coast of Maine. But his talent for ma-

neuvering men proved even more valuable than his seamanship when he went to Washington. After World War I broke out, he played an important role in building the U.S. Navy's fighting strength.

In 1920 he received a reward he would have preferred not getting: He accepted the nomination for the Vice Presidency on the Democratic ticket. He knew it was no prize, for the nation clearly had no intention of choosing his running mate, Governor James Cox of Ohio, as its Chief Executive. Republican Warren G. Harding's promise to "bring back normalcy" won over the nation, as Roosevelt had been gloomily sure it would, and he found himself back in private life, with scant prospect of ever getting another chance at national office.

But his spirits were too bouncy to stay discouraged long. Besides, he had along his political way acquired as confidential aide an ugly gnome of a former newspaperman who was positive he could put Franklin Roosevelt in the White House. With Louis M. Howe loyally pulling strings for him still, Roosevelt settled into private law practice.

Being so full of energy, he had an assortment of other interests as well —business investments, charity drives, yachting expeditions. As usual, his family was up at Campobello in the summer of 1921, and he pushed himself furiously to finish a variety of projects in New York before sailing to join his wife and children. A friend with a good-sized boat had invited him to be a passenger on a cruise to the Canadian island. But storm and fog made the voyage something less than pure pleasure; being the only man aboard experienced in Bay of Fundy waters, FDR took the wheel for hours.

Arriving at Campobello, he kissed the family, changed clothes and went fishing immediately, instead of resting. Out on the water, he was crossing from yacht to tender when he slipped.

"I never felt anything so cold as that water," he recalled later. "I hardly went under, hardly wet my head, because I still had hold of the side of the tender, but the water was so cold it seemed paralyzing."

The next day, the effects of his dunking strangely persisted. But weak as he felt, Roosevelt could not rest. There was a forest fire on a nearby island, and he spent hours cutting evergreen branches to flail at the flames. His older sons had come along, and when they all got back exhausted, he decided the best way to perk up was to swim in the icy bay.

"I didn't feel the usual reaction, the glow I'd expected," Roosevelt remembered afterward. Instead, he was barely able to drag his legs as he went upstairs to rest before dinner.

That was the last time he ever walked unaided.

For the next morning there could be no doubt. This tall, powerful man of thirty-nine could not stand up. His legs were numb; he was at least partly paralyzed from the chest down. It took some time to get experienced doctors to the isolated island. When they came and examined the patient, they nodded bleakly. "Infantile paralysis," they said.

Polio, as it was commonly called, most often struck small children, but adult

Roosevelt with a therapist at Warm Springs.

cases were far from rare. With no known cure, and only small hope for improvement of the paralytic symptoms once they appeared, thousands of victims were dying of polio every year then, and more thousands were being left helplessly crippled. If Franklin D. Roosevelt despaired on hearing the diagnosis of the doctors, he would have had good reason.

But if he ever felt despair, nobody except Eleanor Roosevelt and Louis Howe knew it. Howe had come up to Campobello to talk over some political planning, and he stayed to become, for all his quirky ways and small stature, a tower of strength. He and Roosevelt's wife, who had become a quiet, poised mother of five, refused to give up hope. Night and day, they calmly tended their patient until complex arrangements could be completed for transferring him to a city hospital.

Almost as if they hoped to defy the fates by not admitting how seriously ill Roosevelt was, they did not let anybody else know what the doctors had said. Since his name was nationally known, the arrival of a special train and stretcher-bearers could not be kept secret; but Mrs. Roosevelt announced only

that her husband had a bad case of the flu. Gritting his teeth to keep from showing the pain as he was moved, Roosevelt cooperated with the deception.

Once he had arrived safely in New York City, the truth was told. By then it seemed clear that he would live. But about the paralysis, there could be no reassuring words spoken—except by Roosevelt himself. "I expect it might be a year or two before I can play golf," he said jauntily.

The only fear he would admit was a blind, unreasoning terror that while he was lying helpless, fire might break out in the New York City house where the family was now installed. Rather than merely brood about his fear, though, he took what action he could.

To the indescribable anguish of those who loved him, he spent hours lying on the floor painfully but doggedly teaching himself a sort of crablike crawl, so that he would be able to escape a fire even if no other help could reach him.

Yet the tone in the household was not somber. To make sure his sturdy sons did not pity him, Roosevelt challenged them to wrestling bouts on the floor. The power of his arm and shoulder muscles was such that he could still pin down the boys. Visitors were astonished to find the family engaged in such hilarious rough-and-tumble sport.

Not that Roosevelt did not take his plight seriously. He put every ounce of the will power he had developed over the years into trying to get back at least partial use of his legs. Doctors told him he might be able to stand up with metal leg braces if he could endure the extreme discomfort involved, and he hesitated

not an instant. Heavy leg braces were ordered at once. In time, wearing them and using crutches to propel himself along, he managed a few steps on his own.

Every day he spent hours determinedly exercising his wasted body. The best help of all, he decided in time, was the warm-water swimming he had tried at a rundown resort in Georgia that someone had recommended to him. With his customary energy, he set out rebuilding Warm Springs, Georgia, as a center for treating infantile-paralysis patients.

Investing his own money and begging donations from friends, he succeeded within a few years in establishing a foundation to take on this and related projects. The foundation eventually spurred the research by Dr. Jonas Salk that led to the first success in the quest for a polio vaccine.

Even as Roosevelt was striving day after day just to stand upright with his braces, and even as he was quietly accepting within his own mind that he would never walk again, let alone play golf, he kept in touch with various outside activities. He sent Howe out constantly to see leading political figures; he encouraged his wife to take an active part on political committees. His goal was simply to keep his name before the public. Who said a man in his position could not become President?

His mother said so, for one. She begged him to give up any thought of a further political career, to stay peacefully at Hyde Park. Gently and yet decisively, he refused to let her sway him.

Instead he wrote constantly to political leaders, he had them come visit, in time

FDR nominating Al Smith for President.

he began going out in a wheelchair to attend small private conferences. Because his pluck had won him new respect among the voting public at large, his endorsement became highly desirable, and candidates sought him out. By 1924, the group backing Alfred E. Smith of New York for President had the boldness to suggest a public appearance by Roosevelt. They wanted him to nominate Al Smith for President at the Democratic National Convention.

But how could Roosevelt reach the rostrum? Could he stand with his braces long enough to make a speech? Would the public receive him with pity instead of respect when they saw the effort that merely standing upright cost him?

Brushing aside all such questions, Franklin Roosevelt came before that convention supported by the strong arm of his oldest son. He stood, thanks to his leg braces, without faltering once. And his face beamed a smile that touched millions of hearts.

In a voice of dauntless resonance, Roosevelt nominated Al Smith that evening. But almost everybody who heard him understood that Franklin Roosevelt was doing much more than merely nominating another man for high office. He was proving beyond any possible doubt that he himself was still in the running.

He soon became a serious candidate in his own right. No longer just a rich man with a talent for winning votes, he now had a kinship with the suffering. He seemed more deeply interested in the problems other people faced than he ever had been before being stricken.

Four years after making that speech,

Franklin Roosevelt became the governor of New York. Four years later, in 1932, he was elected U.S. President.

Elected four successive times to that highest office of the American people, serving longer than any other President, leading the nation through the worst depression in its history and the fearsome crisis of World War II, he never once stood upright without suffering pain in silence.

Few men in the whole long sweep of human history have been mourned as was Franklin Delano Roosevelt when he died suddenly on April 12, 1945. He had been hated too in his lifetime, with a rare zeal. Among the rich, many called him a traitor to his class. His new measures for helping the underprivileged—innovations like social security and unemployment benefits—were often damned as un-American. But for the vast majority of the American people, as well as to millions elsewhere, the three initials of FDR had come to symbolize true heroism. "The only thing we have to fear is fear itself," he had told the American people—and by his own courage, he proved it.

AUDIE MURPHY
Most Decorated Serviceman

Just after his seventeenth birthday, a small, skinny boy walked into a Marine recruiting office in Greenville, Texas, near his home. It was June 1942, six months after the Japanese bombed Pearl Harbor and brought the United States into war.

The baby-faced boy with wavy brown hair and grey eyes didn't look like the tough fighting man that the Marines wanted. He was only five feet seven in height, weighing only a little more than a hundred pounds. But he was determined to be a soldier, to get into the war before it was over.

Ever since he had been a much smaller boy, working in the hot sun in the fields of cotton and corn, Audie Leon Murphy had dreamed of the glamorous life of a soldier. The son of a poor farming family that rented land to eke out enough food to live on, Audie had been made tough by hunger and poverty. His father had disappeared when he was a child; his mother had struggled to keep the family of nine boys and girls together.

Frequently, Audie had borrowed a .22-caliber rifle to hunt for rabbits; if he missed, the family didn't eat. Sometimes, when he wasn't able to get a rifle, he used a slingshot to bag rabbits for the stewpot. When his mother died, the Murphy family split up. The younger children went into an orphans' home; Audie decided to enlist.

But the Marine recruiting sergeant looked him over and turned him down. He was too frail for the Marines. Audie tried the paratroops, but they too rejected him. Finally, he crammed himself full of food to build up his weight. He took the physical examination for the Army—and passed. He became one of the twelve million Americans who served in the armed forces during World War II.

At the beginning Audie Murphy wasn't much of a soldier. During his first days of infantry training, after receiving his immunization shots, he fainted on the drill field. The other soldiers began to call him "Baby." The final humiliation came when he was assigned to a cooks' and bakers' school.

"Lock me up, I won't go!" he told his commanding officer. He didn't go. For his pluck he was allowed to stay in the infantry after he completed his basic training.

After combat training, a kindly officer took pity on the boyish-looking soldier and ordered him transferred to a clerk's

Audie and his dog.

job. But Audie rebelled again and remained an infantryman. Sent abroad to North Africa as a replacement soldier, he was assigned to Company B of the 15th Regiment, 3rd Infantry Division.

The war really started for Private Murphy on the beaches of Sicily in July 1943, as the American troops waded ashore. His illusions about the glamor of warfare disappeared quickly as he watched shell explosions and machine-gun fire kill men around him.

Two enemy officers, mounted on white horses, galloped furiously away from an advance party of scouts that included Murphy. He dropped to his knee and, sighting with an eye that was trained to hit targets not much bigger than rabbits, he fired twice. The men rolled over, fell from the horses and lay still.

Audie was good at his job, so good that he was quickly promoted, first to corporal, then to sergeant. At the Anzio beach-

head and up through the boot of Italy, he learned the fine art of survival, despite bombs, mud, bullets and despair. For an infantryman, it was shoot first or be shot, and Audie was quick on the trigger.

In March 1944, while on a patrol probing into German lines in Italy, Audie crept toward a partly disabled Nazi tank. Taking careful aim, he fired several rifle grenades at the tank, destroying it. Under a hail of machine-gun bullets, he led all his men back to the American lines and safety.

For this exploit he received the Bronze Star medal, the first in a long series of awards.

Several months later Audie and his company hit the beaches of Southern France, completing a giant pincer movement around Germany's western front that had begun on D-Day, June 6, 1944, with the invasion of Normandy. Piercing a thin line of resistance, Company B moved inland until it was stopped by intense machine-gun fire.

Leaving his men in a covered position, Audie dashed back forty yards through withering fire until he found a small ditch that led back to the beach. There he picked up a machine gun and, carrying it alone, returned to the front lines. By the time he was ready for action, reinforced by more arms and ammunition, enemy bullets were popping within a foot of him.

In the duel that followed, Audie silenced the enemy weapons, killing all the German soldiers in the trenches in front of the enemy strongpoint. With one other man, he scrambled up to an enemy gun pit and shot its occupants.

94

The Americans ducked as machine-gun fire opened up on them.

"Have you got any idea of how to get out of this spot?" his buddy asked.

"No, I'm open to suggestion," Murphy said.

"We should have looked it up in the field manual."

One thing they did know was that staying put would be suicidal. Heaving hand grenades, the two soldiers jumped up and emptied their carbines into the nearby machine-gun nest. The Germans yelled: "Kamerad"—comrade. But as Audie's buddy arose to accept their surrender, the Germans cut him down.

Alone on the hill, with enemy fire all around him, an angry Audie picked up an enemy machine gun. Firing methodically, he walked slowly up the hill to its summit. Miraculously, none of the enemy fire hit him as he raked the Germans with their own machine gun.

"His extraordinary heroism resulted in the capture of a fiercely contested enemy-held hill and the annihilation or capture of the enemy-held garrison," his citation for a Distinguished Service Cross read. Audie had won the nation's second highest decoration for bravery in battle.

Day after day, as the American forces inched their way north, it was hard fighting. Men around Murphy were killed and wounded; many dropped from exhaustion and battle fatigue. But frail Audie Murphy seemed to lead a charmed life. Finally, on September 15, a mortar shell exploded near him and he was wounded on the foot. He was awarded a Purple Heart for a wound received in action.

Two weeks later, back in the front lines, Audie was visited by the officers commanding the battalion. They wanted to see for themselves what was holding up the American advance. They went forward on a trail up a hill.

Following them a few moments later, Audie heard two grenades explode. Machine-gun bullets rained down the hillside. The Germans obviously had trapped the officers.

With a carbine in his left hand and a grenade in his right, Audie inched up the trail. All seemed quiet. He stepped from behind a rock, lobbing a grenade into the German party. They wheeled around, but Audie was quicker. He fired his carbine and then threw some more grenades into the German position, killing four of them immediately and wounding three others. One German attempted to escape, but Audie shot him down too.

The American commanding officer climbed out of a shallow hole in which he had found some protection from the German fire. He brushed off his uniform.

"Those grenades are not a bad idea," he said calmly. "Next time, I'll bring my own."

For this action, Audie received a Silver Star, the nation's third highest award for bravery. Only three days later, he won another one.

His company was held up by a high point, strategically located and fanatically defended. Dragging a radio with him, Audie crawled fifty yards under German machine-gun fire to a point only a few hundred yards from the enemy. The citation for his medal read:

"Despite machine gun fire and rifle bullets that hit as close as a foot to him, Murphy directed artillery fire upon enemy positions for an hour, killing fifteen Germans and inflicting approximately thirty-five additional casualties. His courage, audacity and accuracy enabled his company to advance and obtain its objectives.''

Constant American pressure forced the Germans to retreat, and the Allied forces paused to reorganize. Three enlisted men, including Audie, were called down to headquarters. All three of them were bearded, dirty, muddy and, like all front-line fighting men, suspicious of the rear-echelon types.

The colonel pinned gold bars on their shoulders, making them lieutenants in the Army of the United States.

"You are now gentlemen by act of Congress," the colonel told them. "Shave, take a bath—and get back into the line."

Thus Audie Murphy, the baby-faced boy now slightly more than nineteen years old, became an officer and a gentleman. Despite his youth, his superior officers recognized that he was an experienced and wise combat leader. His size made no difference now; in the life-and-death test of the front lines, Audie was a big man.

The Germans may have been retreating, but they were still fighting fiercely. On October 26, a bullet hit Murphy on the hip, wounding him severely. He received another Purple Heart for this wound.

It wasn't until January 1945 that he recovered enough to return to his men. The 3rd Division was then fighting along the Rhine River near Strasbourg. The Battle of the Bulge to the north was over and some American units had already entered Germany.

But a large number of Germans, equipped with heavy and efficient tanks, remained on the west, or French, side of the Rhine. They were in an area known as the Colmar Pocket, running south to the Swiss border. It was a threat to the flank of the Allied armies if they attempted to move forward across the Rhine River into the heart of Germany.

In freezing weather, with snow reaching to their knees, the fighting American infantrymen wearily slogged their way over a rickety bridge that crossed the River Ill. Step by step, the men slowly moved forward over the icy fields toward the villages of Holtzwihr and Riedwihr. But as they advanced, the bridge behind them collapsed. No American tanks would be able to follow and help them.

Without support from their own tanks and unable to dig into the frozen ground for cover, the infantrymen were completely without protection when German tanks hit them. Cut to pieces, with wounded and dead men falling to the ground, the survivors fell back.

For two days Murphy's regiment tried to regain the lost ground. On the second day, Murphy's legs were peppered with shrapnel from a mortar blast, but he refused to stop for first aid. By dawn of the third day, Murphy and Company B were at the edge of some woods about a mile from Holtzwihr, with a flat, snow-covered field between them and the village. They were ordered to hold the line. The bridge had finally been repaired, but hardly any American armor had reached the company's forward position.

Company B was out there almost alone. Only two United States tank de-

stroyers were nearby. The murderous enemy fire had cut the company strength from 155 men to about 33. Of the six company officers who had crossed the River Ill, only Audie Murphy was alive and still functioning. Lieutenant Murphy was now the commanding officer of the company he had entered as a raw recruit only two years before. On him was the responsibility of command; on him depended the lives of the men around him.

At 2:00 on the afternoon of January 26, 1945, peering out from the protection of the trees, Murphy saw the Germans lining up for the attack. Six Nazi tanks rumbled out of Holtzwihr, splitting into two teams of three tanks each to attack from both the right and the left. Then wave after wave of tiny white dots —hundreds of German soldiers wearing snowcapes—moved across the silent open field.

One of the American tank destroyers began firing, but then ploughed into a ditch, useless. Its crew jumped out and fled, as the German artillery found the range and pumped shells into the area. One American machine-gun squad was knocked out. A German shell hit the second U.S. tank destroyer, killing two of its men. Black smoke billowed out and swirled across the battlefield.

Despite American artillery fire from far in the rear, the Nazi tanks churned up, raking the American position with machine guns. Resistance was impossible.

"Get the hell out of here," Murphy yelled to the surviving members of his company. "That's an order."

The men fell back reluctantly, leaving Murphy alone. There was nothing be-

tween him and the advancing Germans. His only tie to the rear was a telephone line.

"Keep it coming," he shouted to the artillery men far to the rear.

The shells rained in, but the German infantrymen and tanks kept advancing slowly. They were only about two hundred yards away.

The telephone rang.

"How close are they?" a voice from the rear asked.

"Just hold the phone and I'll let you talk to one of them," Murphy replied.

Firing his carbine until it was empty, Murphy turned to retreat. As he turned, he noticed several boxes of ammunition piled by the turret machine gun on top of the burning tank destroyer. He dragged his telephone over and climbed on. The tank might explode any minute, but at least the Germans would never think of looking for him there. He lay down behind the gun. Firing straight ahead, he saw German infantrymen crumbling in the snow.

He felt the tank destroyer trembling under him. An enemy shell had hit, and black smoke rose once more, obscuring his vision. It was a close call, but a blessing as well. He could not see very well, but the Germans couldn't see him either.

The telephone rang once more.

"Are you still alive, lieutenant?" the voice from the rear asked.

"Momentarily," he said. Then he got back to business. He ordered artillery fire to come fifty yards closer to his tank.

Feeding another belt of cartridges into the machine gun, he fired at anything that moved. But the Germans kept coming, slowly.

"Correct fire, battalion, fifty over," he telephoned back, thus ordering the artillery fire fifty yards still closer to his tank.

"Are you all right, lieutenant?" the rear-echelon voice asked anxiously.

"I'm all right, sergeant," he replied. "And what are *your* postwar plans?"

But there wasn't much more time for jokes. The American artillery fire was now landing within fifty yards of his position, and the Germans were almost there too. Caught in the fire, the Germans slowed down; the Nazi tanks hesitated.

Murphy had one last order.

"Correct fire. Fifty over and keep firing for effect. This is my last change," he telephoned.

"Fifty over?" the sergeant screamed back. "That's your own position."

"I don't give a damn, fifty over," Murphy ordered. The phone went dead. There was nothing more he could do— but the Germans were beginning to turn back.

Murphy carefully put the telephone down. He methodically folded his map, noting that it was riddled with shell fragments. He looked at his arms. No scratches. His right leg throbbed with pain—from the mortar wounds received the day before.

As fire from both the enemy and his own artillery enveloped the tank destroyer, Murphy slowly climbed down, weary and exhausted. Oblivious to the shells bursting all around him, he walked down the road through the forest to the rear, without bothering to run. He heard the tank destroyer explode behind him. Single-handed, he had stopped six Nazi tanks and 250 German troops. But he was beyond caring whether or not he would make it back.

As he walked back, past the bodies of the dead, he began to awake from the stupor of battle. He heard the drone of airplanes in the distance. He began to think, to plan. The Germans were off balance. One more attack and they would be licked.

He rounded up his men and led them forward once more. Hole by hole, grenade by grenade, death by death, Company B pushed forward for the rest of the afternoon, dropping that night to rest in the midst of the bodies of their companions who had fallen earlier in the day. At dawn the village of Holtzwihr was captured.

The Medal of Honor, the nation's highest award for military valor, was awarded to Audie Murphy for his "indomitable courage and his refusal to give an inch of ground which saved his company from possible encirclement and destruction." He also received his third Purple Heart.

Murphy fought with his company until nearly the end of the war; his skill and luck remained with him. Of more than a hundred men who started with Company B in Africa two years before, only

Murphy and a supply sergeant remained on the company rolls when the war ended. All the others had been killed or wounded.

When the fighting stopped, Murphy was honored even more. The United States government awarded him the Legion of Merit for his skill and bravery in commanding Company B.

France made him a member of the Legion of Honor and gave him a Croix de Guerre for his exceptional services in the liberation of France. And Belgium awarded its Croix de Guerre to him.

Altogether, Audie Murphy received twenty-three decorations for his war service, making him the most decorated American fighting man—soldier, sailor or marine—in World War II or, for that matter, any war in the history of the United States.

After the war, Murphy returned home to a hero's welcome in Texas and then the difficult readjustment to civilian life. He had wanted to make the Army his career, but his wounds made that impossible.

On a visit to Hollywood, he took part in a movie. He then got bigger and better roles, until now he is an authentic movie star. But even Audie Murphy admits he is not much of an actor; he plays the roles of soldiers or "good guys" in cowboy pictures where great acting talent is not a must.

He owns several guns, but has gradually given up his old favorite sport of hunting. The idea of killing has receded so much from his mind and his life that he has said: "Now I even hate to cut flowers in the garden."

Audie Murphy after World War II: visiting an American military cemetery (above); and as a movie star in The Red Badge of Courage.

AMELIA EARHART
Heroine of the Skies

Her name was Amelia, which sounded so very ladylike, but she always wanted to try tomboyish things—like galloping furiously on horseback, or belly-whopping on a sled. When other girls were busy with dolls, she built herself a home-made roller coaster.

That was Amelia Earhart during her childhood in Atchison, Kansas, where she was born on July 24, 1898. All through school, she kept wondering how she could settle down to be a proper young lady.

On her ninth birthday, at a state fair, she saw her first airplane, a primitive flying machine with two wings and a box-kite contraption as its tail. She wasn't at all interested then; she was too busy having fun at the fair. But when she was nineteen, working as a nurse's aide in Toronto, the sight of graceful planes making geometric patterns in the sky lured her to an airport at the edge of the city. There she watched longingly as bold young men took their planes into the clouds, and looped, rolled and casually made figure eights in the sky. It was dangerous, but what a challenge!

Then she knew she never would settle down to a placid existence on the ground. Just as she had mastered the galloping

horses as a girl, now she would ride these powerful planes in the vast blue sky. Nothing could stop her from becoming a pilot.

Up till then, she had thought nursing might be the career for her. She had come to Toronto on a visit and stayed to nurse in a hospital for soldiers wounded in the First World War. Even after becoming interested in flying, she thought she might also take up medicine, and in 1919 she began studying at Columbia University as a pre-medical student. Soon afterward, she was in California—learning to fly.

Twelve years later, in 1932, a tiny red airplane stood alone on the runway of the airport at Harbor Grace, Newfoundland, on the edge of the Atlantic Ocean. Its single engine was warming up, its propeller turning. From the edge of a field, a woman bundled in a heavy flying suit walked awkwardly to the plane. She climbed onto the wing and then into the cockpit. After glancing at the instrument panel, she waved to the mechanics on the ground.

"So long!" one of them yelled above the engine's roar. "Good luck!"

Alone in the little red plane, Amelia Earhart taxied to the end of the runway, then paused to check her engine. After listening a few seconds, she let the plane head down the runway, gaining speed. At 7:13 P.M. on the evening of May 20, 1932, she took off—to try to fly across the Atlantic.

No woman had ever before made a solo flight like this. Only five years earlier, almost five years to the day, Charles A. Lindbergh had flown alone from New York to Paris, making aviation history; and solo ocean flights were still considered extraordinarily daring.

But just as in her childhood, Amelia Earhart craved the adventure of tempting the unknown. It had nothing to do with wanting to be a heroine; she simply felt she could not endure missing any of the excitement life had to offer. No matter that she had been born female. She had long since decided that would not stop her.

Already she was famous. Only a year after Lindbergh's historic flight, in 1928, she had tested her nerve by attempting an ocean flight; but on that occasion she was merely a passenger. Even so, the feat put her name in newspapers everywhere.

She took the furor calmly. When a friend in London asked her why she did not seem more thrilled, she said: "I was just baggage, like a sack of potatoes."

Instead of simply allowing things to happen to her, Amelia Earhart wanted to take an active hand in making things happen.

So here she was, some 12,000 feet above the whitecapped ocean, actively seeking to master a great challenge. The regular purr of the engine made a comforting sound as her plane bored through the clouds over the North Atlantic. Sud-

denly the needle on her altimeter, the gauge that measured her height above the water, began to spin peculiarly. It was obviously not working. Now there would be no way of telling how far she was from the water for the rest of the trip. And the clouds were growing thicker. She was flying into a storm.

Here was challenge aplenty, even for Amelia Earhart.

As the weather worsened, the plane's controls grew sluggish. Without the altimeter, she could still tell she was losing height, but how much? Ice forming on the wings made the plane heavy and she had to concentrate on that problem. When she snatched an instant to look out of her window, she saw the ocean waves less than a hundred feet below. She pulled back on her control stick with all her strength.

Through a long night she maneuvered to stay safely above the waves and yet below the icy upper air that froze her wings. As best she could she kept her course due east, where Ireland should be.

As the sun rose, she drank some hot soup from a thermos bottle and relaxed a bit. Although the ice had not completely melted from her wings, she thought she had managed to stay on schedule. But just when the prospect was seeming brighter, a new problem suddenly arose. The exhaust manifold, the pipe that carried out waste gases, began vibrating dangerously—in a way that would surely cause engine trouble very soon. It was immediately clear to her that she could not continue flying much longer.

Still traveling due east, Amelia Earhart anxiously scanned the horizon. If her navigation had been accurate, Ireland must be straight ahead. But would she have time to reach land?

With a sudden stir of hope, she noted a black line in the distance, and it grew larger and larger. It *was* land, dead ahead. There might be no time to seek an airport, but at least she would not have to come down over the water.

In a few minutes she arrived over dry land and spotted railroad tracks below her. Following them, she hoped, would bring her to a city with an airport. But before she could see any sign of a landing field, the expected engine problem developed. She would have to come down as soon as possible. Picking a green pasture, she calmly guided her little plane down onto the ground.

Amelia Earhart had made it across the Atlantic—in fifteen hours and eighteen minutes. She was the first woman to have flown the ocean; she had earned a permanent place among aviation's pioneer pacesetters.

But where was she?

A farmer ran out of his cottage toward the plane. Miss Earhart climbed onto the wing, and if the sight of a woman pilot startled that farmer, her first words proved even more astounding.

"I'm from America," she said. And where, precisely, had she landed?

On gaining sufficient composure to answer, the man told her she was near Londonderry, in northern Ireland. Then, at her request, he took her to find the nearest telephone. Before anything else, she

A grinning Amelia receives a hearty British welcome after her successful flight over the Atlantic.

had to call her husband in New York and tell him she was safe. Besides being Amelia Earhart, the famous aviatrix, she was also Mrs. George Putnam, the wife of a book publisher.

If she had been famous before, that was nothing to the acclaim showered on her after she reached London the next day. Discarding her oil-stained slacks and plaid sportshirt for a new dress and a stylish hat, she was guest of honor at a series of luncheons, dinners and receptions. Tall, slender, rather boyish-looking, she impressed those who met her as modest and unaffected by all the attention.

As far as she was concerned, she had merely proved to herself that she could perform as well as a man in handling an airplane under difficult circumstances; she had demonstrated to the world the equality of her sex in flying. She knew that her flight, daring as it had been, was merely a small step forward in the history of aviation.

"If science advances and aviation progresses and international good will is promoted because of my flight, no one will be more delighted than I—or more surprised," she told an interviewer.

Nevertheless, the world made Miss Earhart a celebrity. She was named an honorary member of the British Guild of Air Pilots and Navigators. The French made her a Knight of the Legion of Honor. In presenting her with this award, France's President said: "Five years ago I had the pleasure to decorate Colonel Lindbergh after his remarkable flight. And now I have the honor to bestow this cross upon the colonel's charming counterpart."

She then returned to the United States by ship. Again following in Lindbergh's footsteps, she was cheered by thousands on her arrival in New York. On June 21, 1932, President Herbert Hoover personally gave her the medal of the National Geographic Society. "The nation is proud," he said, "that an American woman should be the first woman in history to fly an airplane alone across the Atlantic Ocean."

Miss Earhart replied with typical modesty: "I think that the appreciation for the deed is out of proportion to the deed itself. I shall be happy if my small exploit has drawn attention to the fact that women, too, are flying."

Instead of being satisfied with what she had already accomplished, she was already looking for new worlds to conquer. She had never been content with standing pat; she had always kept searching for still another test. Even in high school, her yearbook had described her as "the girl in brown who walks alone."

Now, on returning from London a world-famed heroine, she began planning her next venture. It would be, she decided, a flight from Hawaii to the United States.

No woman had yet flown over the Pacific, and this was the sort of challenge Amelia Earhart could not resist. Her old plane, the one in which she had flown the Atlantic, had already gone to the Franklin Institute in Philadelphia as part of an aeronautics exhibit. She got a new one, also a Lockheed Vega, also painted bright red. On January 11, 1935, she was ready.

She took off from Hawaii late that afternoon and climbed to about 6,000

Amelia inspects her new Lockheed Electra, the plane she chose to take her around the world.

feet, then set her course due east. By radio, she let Honolulu know: "Everything okay." Turning her radio dial, she was listening to music from a Hawaiian station when an announcer broke in to read what he said was an important news flash. "Amelia Earhart has just taken off on an attempted flight to Oakland in California," he reported.

"You're telling me!" Miss Earhart shouted out loud in her little cabin.

That night and the next morning, she had no problems except the basic one of staying awake. Her plane flew beautifully. She watched the sunrise, she scanned the ocean below for any signs of a ship, she searched for the California coastline. Exactly on schedule San Francisco Bay loomed ahead, and she coasted into a landing at Oakland as if she had just completed the most routine milk run.

After that it was one record-breaking flight after another for Amelia Earhart. From Burbank, California, to Mexico City; from Mexico City to Newark, New Jersey. She set a new transcontinental speed record for women by flying across the country in seventeen hours. Nothing seemed too difficult for her.

While planning still other air missions, she also embarked on a new career. Invited to join the faculty of Purdue University, she began working in the aeronautics department and as a guidance counselor for girl students. The advice she gave the girls was: find your own aptitudes, change jobs if something better comes up and, above all, have fun in what you are doing. It was the credo that she herself lived by.

Purdue was so pleased to have Miss Earhart that they set up a fund of $50,000 and bought her an airplane for experimental work. It was a twin-engined, ten-passenger Lockheed transport. Then she began planning her most challenging flight of all—a round-the-world trip along the equator.

This was something nobody had ever done, man or woman. She meant to be the first pilot ever to fly around the world at its widest part. At a press conference in New York she tried to explain why.

"I've seen the North Atlantic," she said, "and I've seen the Pacific, too, of course, at least part of it. Well, just say I want to fly around the globe. And I think that a round-the-world flight just now should be at the equator."

Amelia and Fred Noonan in Brazil during a stop on their round-the-world flight.

On so extensive a mission, she would need a navigator. She chose Frederick J. Noonan, who had worked with Pan American Airlines in pioneering routes across the Pacific. After months of trial runs to test their equipment, a first attempt, east to west, ended with a crack-up in Hawaii. Several months later they were ready to go again. At 5:56 P.M. on June 1, 1937, they took off from Miami —bound for California the long way round.

Their first stop was San Juan in Puerto Rico, then Venezuela, Dutch Guinea and Brazil. Crossing the Atlantic from Brazil, they touched down next at Senegal in Africa. After Africa, the Red Sea, the Arabian Sea, Karachi . . . Singapore . . . Java . . . Timor . . . Australia. On June 30, they flew north to New Guinea where they braced themselves for one of the longest over-the-water hops—to Howland Island, 2,556 miles away.

Howland Island is a dot in the Pacific, about two miles long and a half mile wide. There is nothing between New Guinea and Howland except water and a few small isles. Aids to navigation were limited in 1937, and the plane's radio had a range of only 500 miles, which meant they would be flying blind, or by dead reckoning, most of the way. At the end of the flight, they would have to find that tiny dot to make a safe landing. But a Coast Guard cutter, the *Itasca,* would be there to help with its radio signals.

At 10:00 on the morning of July 2, the plane sped down the runway and up into the air and climbed to 8,000 feet. Miss Earhart set the course for Howland. At 5:20 P.M. she radioed that they were 795 miles out at sea. Early the next morning, the *Itasca* began to send out weather reports. Only once did its radio officer hear Miss Earhart answer: "Cloudy and overcast."

As day broke over the vast Pacific, the *Itasca* kept trying to reach the plane. Suddenly at 6:45 a signal came through from Miss Earhart: "Please take a bearing on us." Obviously the plane was lost. If it had been on course, it would be near Howland; but it was not. Just before 8:00 A.M., when she should have been landing at Howland, Miss Earhart came through once more by radio: "We are circling, but cannot hear you."

"Will you please come in and answer?" the *Itasca* radioed back immediately.

Silence.

The *Itasca* repeated the query.

Forty-five minutes later, the cruiser's radio picked up the voice of Miss Earhart, obviously distressed: "We are running north and south."

That was the last message from Amelia Earhart and Fred Noonan. The *Itasca* tried for hours to reach them, but there was no response. It became clear that the plane's fuel must have run out, and it must be down somewhere in the Pacific, somewhere in an area of almost half a million square miles.

The United States Navy then dispatched an aircraft carrier, a battleship, four destroyers and other ships to search as thoroughly as possible. For sixteen days, ships and Navy planes crisscrossed, looking for any sign of the Electra.

No trace of the plane or of the two fliers ever was found. The official explanation was that the plane had been lost at sea. But even today, some people refuse to accept this. They believe that Miss Earhart was on a secret spying mission for the United States government to explore the Japanese-held islands of the Pacific and to report back on their military installations. According to these stories, which have never been proved or decisively disproved either, the Earhart plane came down near one of these Japanese-occupied islands, where Fred Noonan was later executed and Miss Earhart died of dysentery.

Whatever the merits of this theory, it is a fact that Amelia Earhart disappeared somewhere in the South Pacific in July of 1937, at the age of thirty-nine. But her story lives on, the story of a pioneer in aviation, a woman who proved that her sex was no barrier to accomplishment, a pilot whose courage was equal to the challenges of the unknown.

Amelia's stepson and husband await word of the missing plane.

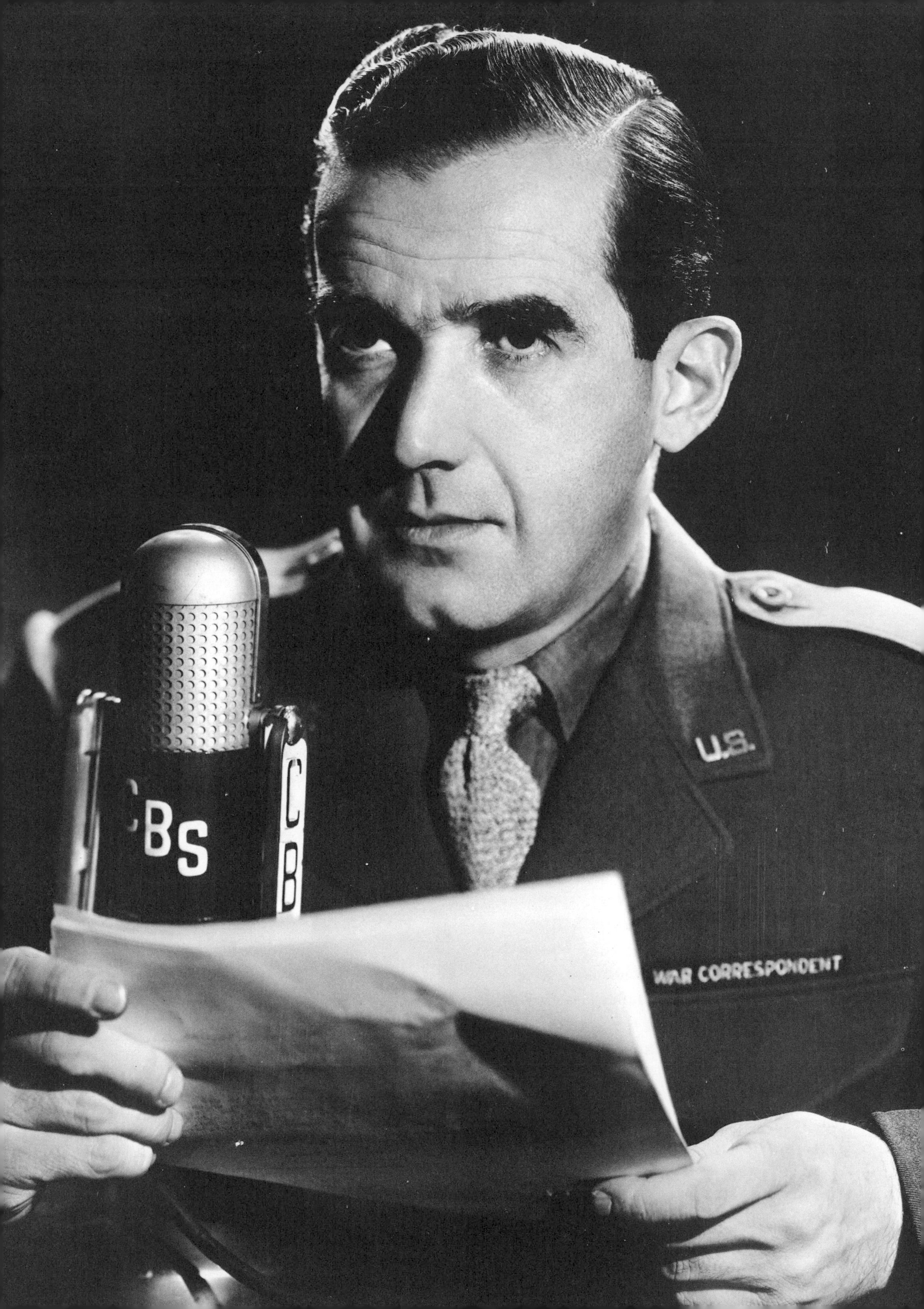
CBS
CB
U.S.
WAR CORRESPONDENT

EDWARD R. MURROW
Voice of America

"This . . . is London."

The calm, deep voice of Edward R. Murrow was speaking to America, by radio. It was 1940, and World War II was not yet a year old.

In living rooms throughout the United States, parents hushed their children. Chairs were drawn closer. The task of doing the supper dishes paused.

Ed Murrow told his millions of listeners about walking back to his apartment from the broadcasting studio the preceding evening, just after one of the biggest bombing raids had ended. "The windows in the West End were red with reflected fire," he said, "and the raindrops were like blood on the panes."

All over an America that was still safe from the firsthand horror of war, the words brought home a vivid picture of what was happening to the proud old capital of Great Britain. Germany had invaded Poland in September of 1939 and conquered it with a new kind of lightning attack, called a blitzkrieg. Nazi tanks and troops, supported by wave on wave of screeching dive bombers, had then turned on France; and France surrendered. Now it was England's turn. Day after day, night after night, German planes were trying to bomb stubborn England into submission.

"The antiaircraft barrage has been fierce," Ed Murrow reported, "but sometimes there have been periods of twenty minutes when London has been silent. That silence is almost as hard to bear."

Americans who could not wait for their morning newspapers to find out if England was still fighting back had to rely then on radio, for television had not yet come into general use. There were many American radiomen in London during those early days of the war. But none could match the black-haired young Murrow in conveying the feelings aroused by the war, as well as the facts. Nobody else, no diplomat or writer, did as much to give the people of the United States a sense of closeness to the terrible drama taking place in Britain.

Without any question, Ed Murrow would have scoffed at the idea that he and the other reporters were heroes. What if he was braving bombs every day? So were millions of Londoners. Like them, he got up every morning to do his job as best he could, despite the inconvenience of air raids—that was all he would admit.

But Murrow was doing a job of immense importance to the whole free world. His skill at catching the spirit of England at war and communicating so

War-torn London as Murrow saw it in 1940.

eloquently what he saw played a major part in building American sympathy for the British cause; it did much to bolster American determination that Hitler's dictatorship must not be allowed to rule the earth.

Murrow's heroism was the quiet sort, just as his words and manner were. For instance, on the night after the Germans bombed Buckingham Palace:

"When friends and relatives have been killed," he told America, "when you've seen that red glow in the sky night after night, when you're tired and sleepy—there isn't enough energy left to be outraged about the bombing of a palace. The king and queen have earned the respect and admiration of the nation, but so have tens of thousands of humble folk who are much less well protected."

It took a high order of reporting talent, along with great personal courage, to cover this kind of battle, and Murrow had both.

Thirty-three years old at the time, he had been born near Greensboro, North Carolina, on April 25, 1908. The first test of his bravery came early; his parents had named him Egbert. Any boy who could live with the teasing that came of having a name like that had at least the makings of a hero.

When he was six years old, his family moved to the state of Washington, where his father worked as a railroad engineer for a logging company. Young Egbert attended Washington State University, and he showed there that common sense sometimes is the greater part of valor; he changed his name from Egbert to Edward.

Whether or not the change had anything to do with it, Ed Murrow made an outstanding record at college. He graduated in 1930 as president of the student body and top man in the student military training unit. Never one to brag, he made light of it when he was also tapped by Phi Beta Kappa, the national honor society limited to college students with the highest marks.

But despite the promise he showed, Murrow had a hard time after he left college during the depth of the Great Depression. His first jobs were for the National Student Federation and the Institute of International Education, both of which paid little; but they did provide the opportunity for getting acquainted with Europe.

Then in 1935, the Columbia Broadcasting System hired Murrow as its director of education. His assignment was merely to speak before various groups about the importance of radio as an educational medium.

110

Two years later, further opportunity opened to him when CBS sent him to Europe as a one-man staff in charge of arranging cultural programs. But Europe was changing in the late 1930's, and so Ed Murrow's job changed too. When Hitler marched into Austria in 1938, Murrow chartered a plane to reach Vienna in time to report the arrival of Nazi soldiers. It was his debut as a war correspondent.

This was a role he relished. As he himself put it later, he found himself with "a front-row seat for some of the greatest news events of history." He proved no ordinary spectator.

His warm faith in the democratic way would not let him miss any chance to warn of the perils building in Europe. Not the least bit pompous, he never said he felt he had a mission to inform America of the truth about Hitler; but that is what he did.

And when the war came, Murrow personally made sure his front-row seat was a traveling seat. He broadcast eyewitness accounts of air raids from rooftops; he boarded a minesweeper to report on naval operations—his superiors had firmly forbidden that exploit because of the danger involved, but Murrow ignored them. He also flew twenty-five combat missions, despite the opposition of his bosses, who regarded him as too valuable to be risked. But like all war correspondents, he took a fatalistic view. To him, danger was everywhere; there could be no point in trying to avoid it. His office in London was bombed out three times, but he escaped without injury.

Murrow's broadcasts from London,

Murrow on his way to work.

then North Africa, then finally the continent of Europe after D-Day in 1944, gripped listeners by their tone as much as their content. It was a grave tone, varied with well-timed pauses. One of his colleagues remarked with some truth that Ed always gave the impression that he knew the worst.

After the war, Ed Murrow returned to the United States—and a big promotion. He was made a vice president of CBS, in charge of all news, education and discussion programs. But he soon found that the tasks of an executive were not for him. He hated endless conferences and memos and little wire baskets for in and out mail. After eighteen months, he was back on the air. "I wanted to be a reporter again," he explained simply.

In September 1947, he began his new program, called "Edward R. Murrow With the News." It was carried by 125 stations to an audience of several million, who became familiar with the opening, "This . . . is the News," and the crisp closing, "Good night and good luck." As successful in peace as he had been in war, Murrow soon was earning more than $100,000 a year.

As television gradually replaced radio, Murrow made the transition with ease and became even more popular. His

Visiting the Korean battlefront, Murrow (right) talks with soldiers about home.

earnings grew rapidly and more than doubled, and so did his influence. He and a colleague, Fred W. Friendly, inaugurated a news program called "See it Now" in November 1951. And the nation began to recognize the face as well as the voice. They saw a high-domed forehead, deep-set serious eyes and constantly knitted eyebrows. A cigarette in Murrow's hand became a sort of trademark.

One of the most important television shows he did came on December 28, 1952. It was called "This . . . is Korea, Christmas 1952." He tried, as he had in London, to present the face of war and of the men who fought in it—but this time with pictures as well as words. Individual soldiers of all nations told why they were fighting and sent messages to their homes. One critic called it "one of the most impressive presentations in television's short life."

But this critical success was dwarfed by another show he did on March 10, 1954. Demonstrating that he could not care less if he made enemies in a cause he believed was right, he examined the phenomenon known as McCarthyism, a highly controversial subject. In those early days of television, controversy was always avoided. Television was considered to be an entertainment medium; the television networks believed that controversial topics were too hot to handle.

Senator Joseph R. McCarthy, a Republican from Wisconsin, was then at the height of his crusade against Communists and Communist influence in the United States. Some people regarded this highly publicized drive as a hard

search for subversives by a zealous patriot. Others saw it as dangerous trickery, taking advantage of an issue for the purpose of gaining political influence by frightening any who dared to disagree. There were many vocal supporters of McCarthy who believed any tactics against Communism should be supported. Few people dared speak out openly in opposition to McCarthy, even though they feared he was abusing the Constitution and the Bill of Rights.

Murrow and Friendly broke the television habit of avoiding controversy. Using film clips that showed McCarthy at his worst, they examined the man and his methods. They showed him making charges that Communists had infiltrated the government—and they showed him failing to prove his charges.

The program had a devastating effect, and McCarthyism lost force in the following months. Of course, that was not due only to the television show. Throughout the country, other people were taking heart at the example of Murrow and a few other courageous Americans. More people began to speak out against smear tactics. "The timing was right and the instrument was powerful," Murrow said modestly of his own show.

But the television critic of *The New York Times,* Jack Gould, had another viewpoint. "Murrow decided to go ahead at a time when passions in the broadcasting industry were running wild on the issue of Communist sympathizers and dupes," Gould wrote. And Murrow had insisted on the freedom to do his news shows as he saw fit, despite the pressures for conformity both within the network and outside. He thus gained a measure

113

Murrow at the dedication of a Voice of America radio station.

of freedom for all of television.

He won the Peabody Awards for excellence in broadcasting in 1943, 1949, 1951 and 1954. William Paley, president of CBS, called him "a man fitted for his time and task—a student, a philosopher and at heart a poet of mankind and, therefore, a great reporter." Murrow took a lighter tone about his own career. "My father did not go so far as to say there's something dishonest about a man making a living by talking," he once remarked, "but he did think there was something dubious about it."

When John F. Kennedy was elected President of the United States in 1960, he selected Murrow, the nation's best-known network commentator, to be director of the United States Information Agency, the government agency in charge of telling America's story overseas. Murrow's salary fell to $21,000 a year—one-tenth of what it had been. He took the job in January 1961, ending a 25-year association with CBS. He now faced the challenge that most reporters duck: could he do a better job of planning official news broadcasts than he had done as a critic of such programs in the past?

He put his reporter's credo to work at once. He believed that facts were more persuasive than propaganda and he told USIA writers to report the news in perspective, the bad as well as the good. He defended the agency's policy of distributing news of racial violence in this country. Such events cannot be kept secret, he said. There was no choice but to present the facts with balanced interpretation.

When members of Congress criticized his staff for not depicting everything about the U.S. in rosy terms, Murrow replied simply: "We cannot make good news with bad practice."

From Washington, Murrow directed the output of news for 789 weekly hours of broadcasting and in the daily file of 10,000 words to newspapers in a hundred cities overseas. In 1963 the agency sought more money, but its budget was cut. Murrow said that the cut denied the United States a chance to compete on equal terms with the Communists in the struggle of conflicting ideologies. "If we fail, history will take its revenge," he said.

A year later, suffering from cancer, he resigned and returned to New York. He died in 1965 at the age of fifty-seven. But Ed Murrow will be remembered as an honest and courageous journalist who reported the facts as he saw them, a hero who demonstrated to the world how the powerful new communication tools of radio and television could be wisely used in the interests of freedom.

Ed Murrow with his son at his Connecticut farm.

WILLIAM J. DONOVAN
Master of Spies

"When in serious trouble, it's a good idea to send for Bill Donovan," President Franklin D. Roosevelt used to say.

The United States was in serious trouble in January 1942. Scarcely a month before, on December 7, Japanese planes had attacked Pearl Harbor. Reeling from a series of unexpected defeats, America was falling back in the Philippines; at home, the nation was united but unprepared for war. Clearly, there was a long hard road ahead before the United States could muster its armed forces and convert its industrial might into military strength.

At the White House, President Roosevelt and his chief aides were concerned about the gaps in our information about the enemy. Taken by complete surprise at Pearl Harbor, the American military forces had failed in one of their major missions—anticipating what any potential enemy was planning. If we were to win the war, one of the necessary—and immediate—steps must be to build up a reliable intelligence network.

The man the President turned to was William Joseph Donovan, a soft-spoken, grey-haired, blue-eyed lawyer. Bill Donovan was also a Latin scholar, a baseball and fight fan and one of the nation's

leading military heroes of World War I. He had been born in Buffalo, New York, on New Year's Day, 1883. He graduated from Columbia College, where he played football. Then he got his law degree at Columbia Law School, where one of his classmates and friends was a rich young man named Franklin Roosevelt.

Back home in Buffalo, Donovan began a law practice and also enlisted in the New York National Guard. Ten years later, when the United States declared war on Germany in 1917, Donovan went overseas as a captain in the Rainbow Division, the first American troops to land in France. Training rookies one morning, after an exhausting practice march, he pointed to a hill nearby.

"Now, we run to the top of that hill," he ordered.

There was grumbling in the ranks. The men were tired and wanted a rest.

"I've got fifty pounds on my back the same as each of you and I'm twenty years older than any of you boys," Donovan said.

"Yeah," a plaintive voice from the ranks replied, "but we ain't as wild as you are, Bill."

The nickname of "Wild Bill" stuck with Donovan as he established a repu-

Lt. Colonel Donovan of the "Fighting 69th." He is wearing ribbons of the Distinguished Service Cross and the French Croix de Guerre.

tation for incredible bravery during the fighting in France. Later he became commanding officer of the 165th Infantry Regiment, which had been better known earlier as the "Fighting 69th."

Time after time, as the Americans attacked, Wild Bill Donovan climbed out of the trenches ahead of his men into a hail of German machine-gun bullets and shellfire. Yelling at the top of his lungs, he cried: "Come on, boys, come on! They can't hit me—so they can't hit you."

The troops followed him. Father Francis Duffy, the chaplain of the Fighting 69th, once said: "His men would have cheerfully followed him to hell. And as a priest, I mean what I say."

But Wild Bill was not invulnerable. He was wounded in action three times, the last time in October 1918, while directing his regiment in the Meuse-Argonne offensive. Hit in the leg by a machine-gun bullet, he refused to be taken to the rear for medical treatment.

Lying pale and weak on a stretcher, Donovan retained command of his troops and issued orders until their mission was completed. For this he received the Medal of Honor, the nation's highest military award. He already had won the Distinguished Service Cross and the Distinguished Service Medal. The citation for the Medal of Honor read:

"Colonel Donovan personally led the assaulting wave in an attack upon a very strongly organized position, and when our troops were suffering heavy casualties, he encouraged all near him by his example, moving among his men in exposed positions, reorganizing decimated platoons, and accompanying them forward in attacks."

After the war Donovan returned to Buffalo, to his law practice and to public service. He became United States Attorney for the Western District of New York and he served on various government commissions. He ran as the Republican candidate for governor of New York in 1932, but lost.

With the growth of fascism and Nazism in Europe in the mid-1930's, Donovan became convinced that another war was coming. Without any official government position, he went abroad to see for himself.

When the Italians invaded Ethiopia in 1935, Mussolini was reluctant to permit foreign observers at the battlefront. To persuade the pompous Italian dictator, Donovan said: "If you with your genius have re-created the Sixth or the

Tenth Legions of Julius Caesar, then the balance of world politics may be changed."

"You will see for yourself," Mussolini said, beaming.

Donovan went to Ethiopia, saw the Italian armies in action and promptly reported back to military authorities in Washington.

In 1938 he went to Spain to observe the fighting in the civil war there. The Germans, who were supporting the rebel armies of General Francisco Franco, had a new cannon, the 88, later to become one of their most dreaded weapons. Donovan became convinced that the Nazis were using the Spanish civil war as a testing laboratory for this and other new weapons in preparation for their

Donovan and his wife just before his nomination for governor of New York.

next attempt to conquer the world. He so reported to his old friend and classmate, who was now the President of the United States.

Shortly after the Nazis invaded Poland in 1939, touching off the world war that he had foreseen, Donovan again went overseas, this time as an unofficial representative of the United States. It was the summer of 1940; the Battle of Britain was at its height. Already France had fallen, and the Germans were sending waves of bombers and fighters over England in an attempt to pound the stubborn British into submission. Could they survive?

The British showed Donovan everything they had—their radar, their new Spitfire and Hurricane fighters, their coastal defenses, their plans. Donovan returned to the United States with a report that contradicted most other American military intelligence. He was convinced that the British would hold firm, that they would repel the German air attack—and even an invasion, if that should come about.

His analysis was correct; the British won the Battle of Britain and the Germans never even attempted to invade England. President Roosevelt could now point to far more reason than old friendship for relying on Bill Donovan.

In July 1941, Roosevelt appointed Donovan to the post of Coordinator of War Information. Donovan was to analyze and correlate military intelligence and report to the President. Both the Army and the Navy had services gathering information; unfortunately, these services were treated as stepchildren by the military brass. The inadequacy of existing programs was more than proved by Pearl Harbor.

"We have no intelligence service," said the President after Pearl Harbor. That was not completely true; what was lacking was a reliable central intelligence agency. So the President turned to Wild Bill Donovan and asked him to organize a new intelligence service, geared to fight the globar war. On June 13, 1942, the Office of Strategic Services was created, with Donovan as its director.

Donovan knew that it was important to fight the Nazis with the same espionage weapons that they were using against the Allies. Within a matter of months Donovan organized the nucleus of a world-wide organization that eventually was to create terror and disaster behind enemy lines. He recruited scholars and college presidents, bankers and thieves, playboys and professors, debutantes and elderly widows, millionaires and card-carrying Communists.

"Every man or woman who can hurt the Hun is okay with me," he explained.

There were some who criticized the OSS as being too honeycombed with Ivy League types. The wits in Washington called it "Oh, So Social" and "Oh, So Silly."

But Donovan and his recruits were hard workers, creating a brand-new kind of organization with a purpose and secrecy that were basically alien to the American way of life. The OSS had two major functions—sabotage and the collection of information, both equally important. Donovan's organization grew to 12,000 men and women, operating in all theaters of the war (except one: the area under the command of General MacArthur, who preferred to keep all operations under his own control).

In a Washington mansion the research and analysis section sifted information, most of it seemingly unimportant until it was put together. Scholarly workers, skilled in language and interpretation, collected road maps, geological soil data, railroad timetables, letters, old newspapers and books—and came up with astonishingly accurate military information that was invaluable to soldiers in the field.

One agent in Austria, for example, sent in a new freight-rate schedule for a railroad line. An analyst in Washington noted that oil shipment prices were quoted for a tiny Austrian village. His conclusion: a new oil refinery had been built there to hide it from Allied planes. In a few days, Allied bombers flew overhead and wiped it out.

From London, a young Frenchman recruited by the OSS parachuted into France and made his way to Paris. Acting as a deaf-mute to forestall questions about his past, he got a job as a janitor in the Gestapo headquarters there, the very center of the German counterespionage system. For months he gathered information, bicycling out to the country on weekends to radio his data back to London. And then one day, there was silence. One of 200 radio-equipped OSS agents who parachuted into German-held territory to ferret out information, he was one of the few who were caught, captured, tortured and executed.

The successes of the OSS agents were many, but so were their failures. For example, fifteen agents, many of them Italian-Americans from New York, jumped into Northern Italy to dynamite a railroad tunnel. Surprised by the Germans, they were caught and executed on the spot.

OSS agents cooperated with local guerrilla fighters in almost every enemy-occupied country—in Norway, Yugoslavia, Greece, Italy, France, Belgium, Burma—bringing them arms, ammunition and money. The agents' mission in these lands was to fight, to kill, to wreck enemy installations and to maintain morale by their presence and their im-

plicit promise that the Allies were coming to liberate the captured countries.

In 1942 twenty OSS men parachuted into northern Burma and organized the naked, monkey-eating tribe of Kachins to fight the Japanese. Together, the small group of Americans and the larger number of Kachin tribesmen eliminated more than 5000 Japanese soldiers.

In Greece, six American OSS men led an uprising that liberated a large area and caused nearly a thousand Germans to surrender. In Norway, OSS units helped Norwegians blow up railroad

Conference in Burma: (left to right) U.S. Generals Sultan and Wedemeyer, Admiral Lord Mountbatten, and General Donovan.

bridges. In Bavaria, an agent disguised as a German army sergeant was suddenly ordered to check the credentials of German soldiers on a troop train. He found that more than half were traveling without leave and turned them in for disciplinary action.

Back in Washington, Donovan and his assistants worked quietly and efficiently to plan operations of this type. As a lawyer, Donovan had been known as a master of careful preparation; he became an expert in any field he was consulted on. As a spy master, Donovan brought these methodical habits with him. He knew that painstaking care and attention to detail were among the secrets of successful spying.

"You can find out anything you want to know about anybody, if you really work," he used to say.

Using information brought back from the field, his assistants in Washington set up an elaborate counterfeiting plant. They forged documents that could fool the Nazis; they manufactured ration coupons that were accepted without question; they made all kinds of foreign money. They also invented clever new instruments of destruction.

Donovan delighted in deadly pranks. One of his chief assistants was called "Professor Moriarty," after the evil genius who bedeviled Sherlock Holmes. His job was to invent new and devastating devices for agents in the field.

Among these was an electric eye explosive, called "Casey Jones," that would go off only when a train entered a tunnel, thus not only destroying the train, but blocking the tunnel as well. Another was a kind of TNT that looked like flour and was just as harmless when carried as a powder. But when it was kneaded into dough, it became a deadly explosive.

Professor Moriarty and his men made tiny time bombs that could be hidden in a briefcase. They made pointed, pronged devices that resembled jacks used in children's games, but these "jacks" were used to cut truck tires. The OSS also invented a one-shot pistol that looked like a broken pencil stub; an agent captured in France used it to fire the one shot he needed to escape.

Another device was a sort of firecracker that shrieked like a falling bomb before it went off with a roar. It was harmless, but its purpose was to create confusion during which a captured agent could disappear.

Donovan inspired the confidence of his men. His agents were more important to him than meetings. Once, an aide found him talking to a seedy-looking man with a foreign accent, and tried to get him to leave for a meeting at the Pentagon.

"Never mind," Donovan said. "That man is going to jump into Berlin pretty soon. The meeting isn't going anywhere; it can wait."

Careful as he was in preparation, Donovan was impulsive in action, as his own war record showed. He frequently called a member of his staff and said: "Let's go see for ourselves." And off they would go to London or some other war center. No matter what time of day or night he returned, Donovan was at his desk at 8:00 the next morning, seemingly fresh and ready for some new project.

A man with an idea, no matter what

his rank, always had precedence over the brass. Nothing is impossible, was Donovan's motto. "Let's give it a try" was one of his favorite expressions.

Once, at a staff meeting, a young officer who was tired of the slow pace of the war said: "Why don't we just drop into Berlin and assassinate Hitler? It would all be much simpler."

"Well," said Donovan, after a long pause, "why don't we?"

The idea was abandoned after a report was received from Germany that a group of German army officers was hatching an assassination plot without any outside help.

The news of that plot—and its failure —came from Donovan's chief agent in Switzerland, Allen Dulles. From his listening posts in the key neutral country, Dulles had organized an efficient network of information in both Germany and Italy. Dulles was involved in one of the major intelligence coups of the war, negotiating with Nazi generals for the surrender of all German forces in Italy.

Throughout the war, Donovan had agents at the top levels in Germany, in its military staff, the foreign office and even the dreaded Gestapo. The information that came back to Washington, which in turn was fed to the military commanders, was an important factor in the success of the American and Allied military forces in the war.

General of the Army Dwight D. Eisenhower, Supreme Allied Commander, said at the end of the war that a considerable part of the victory was due to "the disruption of enemy rail communications, the harassing of German road moves and the continual and increas-

A hero's welcome: Dwight Eisenhower greeting William Donovan.

ing strain placed on the German war economy and internal services" by the resistance forces, helped by the OSS.

Donovan, promoted to the rank of major general, received a large number of medals for his work—another Distinguished Service Medal, and British, French and Italian honors. He helped prosecute Nazi war criminals at Nuremberg. In 1953 President Eisenhower appointed him Ambassador to Thailand; in 1957 he received still another medal, the National Security Medal (awarded for intelligence services).

Wild Bill Donovan died in 1959. After a career of active service in two World Wars, his name was a symbol of courage and commitment in facing up to the necessary tasks of war—in the command post as well as on the battlefield.

CARRIE CHAPMAN CATT
Crusader for Women Voters

Carrie Lane was going to a one-room school, not far from the Iowa farm where her family had settled. At the age of eleven, she was tall for her years, with long, light-brown hair, blue eyes, and a determined chin like her father's. She also had her mother's sense of humor.

She proved that at school one fine spring day when some of the older boys, among them her brother, scared the girls with a snake. Along with the other girls, Carrie ran screeching out of the schoolyard at the sight of the snake; but then she stopped to think.

If the snake could do harm, those boys would not be so free and easy with it, she thought. The prospect of handling a snake certainly did not appeal to her, but she set her chin firmly and decided: the boys had better be taught a lesson.

She got up early the next morning and looked till she found the same sort of snake. Holding it behind her back, she waited for her brother, Charlie. When he appeared, she suddenly whipped the snake under his eyes. No matter that he was three years older than she and a boy in the bargain—Charlie ran as if a prairie wolf were chasing him. That would show him, Carrie decided gaily.

But two years later, the laugh was on Carrie. It was 1872, the year of an election for President of the United States, and quite some excitement had been stirred up in that part of the country over the political campaign.

The Lanes were relative newcomers to Iowa, having come there after the end of the Civil War. That was when Carrie's father had got the western fever again; already it had taken him from New York State clear out to Wisconsin, where she had been born on January 9, 1859. Once in Iowa, though, on a prairie farm near a town called Charles City, Mr. Lane used some of his extra energy to attend political meetings.

So it happened that Carrie heard a good bit about the campaign in which newspaper editor Horace Greeley, the Democratic candidate, was trying to prevent General Ulysses S. Grant from winning a second term in the White House. Mr. Greeley was her father's candidate —and became Carrie's too. Her feelings on the subject reached such a pitch that she named her new kitten after the editor who wanted to be President.

When Election Day dawned and Carrie went down to the kitchen, she was startled to see her mother wearing an everyday dress.

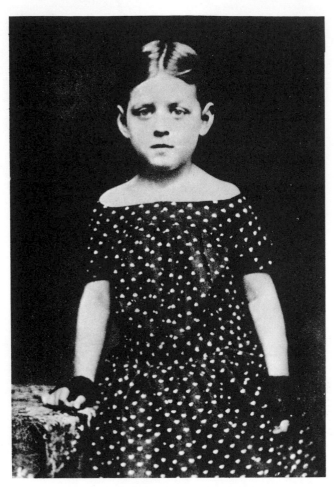

Carrie as a schoolgirl.

"Mother, you're not going to town in that dress, are you?" Carrie said.

"No, I was not thinking of going to town," Mrs. Lane answered calmly.

Carrie looked at her mother, shocked. "Why, Mother, aren't you going to vote for Mr. Greeley?" she demanded.

At that, shouts of laughter filled the kitchen. Brother Charlie and the hired man and Mr. Lane and even Mrs. Lane laughed as if they had just heard the world's best joke. The men were still grinning as they climbed onto the wagon to ride into town and vote.

Then Mrs. Lane explained to her daughter that only men could vote. Women had no part in politics, they never had and never would. Their menfolk voted for them.

Right then in that Iowa farm kitchen, Carrie Lane set her chin and decided: here was something that would have to be changed.

Even at thirteen, she felt just as well qualified as any boy to say what was right. She got better marks in school than any boy did, she could recite in a clear voice without mumbling or stuttering the way most boys did. Yet when she grew up she was to have no say about how the country was run? Carrie shook her head decisively. Such a state of affairs was much too unjust to be allowed to continue.

But it was some time before she began seriously working to end the injustice she felt so strongly. First there was high school, with Carrie riding five miles to town and five miles back again on horseback every day, except in the winter months when her father allowed her to board with a town family. Then, after a stint of teaching in a local school to earn some money, she went to college.

Not many girls even thought of going to college in those days, but Carrie was so positive she wanted all the education she could get that her family made no objection when she offered to earn her own way—by teaching, and later by washing dishes and assisting the librarian, while she attended classes at Iowa State.

After graduation in 1880, she wanted to study law. But within a year after starting law school, she received a telegram offering a tempting job. Although she was scarcely twenty-two, a school district near Charles City wanted her as its high-school principal. Putting on her severest look to awe the students into behaving, she took charge of the school —until she had occasion to bring some notes about an assembly program into the local newspaper office.

The paper had just been bought by a handsome young man named Leo Chapman, who thought at his first sight of Miss Lane that he had never seen a handsomer woman. Two weeks later, they became engaged. It was as Mrs. Carrie Chapman that the former principal began actively working to win the vote for America's women.

As a beginning, she had the notion of convincing Iowa's legislature to grant the vote in local elections to the women of Mason City, where she was living. All

At twenty-two, Carrie was one of the few women of her time to enroll in law school.

on her own, young Mrs. Chapman got a petition started, and before she was finished all but twelve women in Mason City had signed it. Iowa's legislature was astonished—and so was the Iowa Woman Suffrage Association.

Who was this young woman with such wonderful organizing talent? The question buzzed through the ranks of the association—a small, serious-minded group made up mainly of older women striving in a ladylike way to arouse some interest in the cause sponsored by Susan B. Anthony.

That cause was woman suffrage, as the extension of voting rights to women was formally described. Miss Anthony, already more than sixty years old, had gathered a few thousand devoted followers in various parts of the country who had been working more than thirty years, without much success, to extend full citizenship privileges to women.

Delighted that a new recruit had turned up, the Iowa suffrage group invited Mrs. Chapman to a meeting in Cedar Rapids. That, in a real sense, marked a turning point in American history.

The brisk young Mrs. Chapman had none of the air of discouragement that infected older suffrage workers. Standing up in Cedar Rapids to make her first speech, she spoke confidently of the future. What if powerful enemies opposed votes for women? No force could stop progress, Mrs. Chapman assured her audience.

Still, neither she nor the cause was quite ready to burst onto the national scene. Because Mr. Chapman thought newspaper opportunities would be rosier in California, he set out to explore the chances for moving, and his wife had to consider what it would be like to leave her Iowa family and friends. Then once again, a telegram changed her life. From San Francisco she received word that her husband had come down with a severe case of typhoid fever. Even before she could get to San Francisco to care for him, he died.

Too grief-stricken to make plans for her future, she stayed in San Francisco a year, supporting herself with an office job. That gave the widowed Mrs. Chapman a first-hand view of how hard was the lot of the working woman, with all but the lowest-paying jobs closed to her. But mere drifting could not suit Mrs. Chapman long. By the end of the year, an inner voice directed her: go back home to Iowa, and work there to help all women.

The Iowa Suffrage Association welcomed her warmly and appointed her as organizer of new suffrage clubs all over the state. Later she even arranged a regional convention, and that brought her to the attention of Susan B. Anthony herself.

Miss Anthony had spoken at dozens of suffrage conventions over the years, traveling by river boat and stagecoach, by railroad and even on foot. These meetings had one thing in common: in just about every case, Miss Anthony herself raised money to hire a hall and arranged for posters to advertise the meeting. Yet, in Iowa, here was a large meeting carefully and efficiently organized in advance by somebody else. Miss Anthony marveled—and acted. She took this energetic young Mrs. Chapman

under her own wing.

The two traveled together, raising money for the suffrage cause and trying to convert new recruits. If Mrs. Chapman was amazed at times to think that she was working so closely with one of the most famous women America had yet produced, still she realized that "Aunt Susan" needed her. Approaching seventy, even the tireless Miss Anthony was coming near the end of her strength. With a good strong cup of coffee at dinner, she could speak at an evening meeting for half an hour; but lacking the coffee, she would find her voice faltering after only five minutes or so. Then Mrs. Chapman would competently take over. It was matchless training. There seemed little doubt that Aunt Susan wanted her young friend from Iowa to be her succes-

Carrie addressing a suffrage meeting.

sor as president of the National Woman Suffrage Association.

But not till she was eighty did Miss Anthony step down as leader of the association. That happened in 1900, after the status of Mrs. Chapman had changed once more. An engineer named George W. Catt, whom she had met first at college, had convinced her to marry again. Had Mr. Catt not been a most determined sort of man, he never would have persuaded her. After the shock of her first husband's death, Mrs. Chapman had decided marriage was not for her; instead she would devote her life to the suffrage cause.

So Mr. Catt proposed quite solemnly that they form a partnership. He would earn the money for both of them, and she could do the public service for both of them. If she chose to concentrate on promoting woman suffrage as their contribution to the general welfare, that was all right with him; he thought giving the vote to women was an excellent idea. In fact, he even had his lawyer draw up a formal contract stating that for two months every spring and two months every autumn she could travel wherever she wished on suffrage business.

Mrs. Chapman could resist no longer when she read this extraordinary document. She signed it—and was soon planting roses out in back of her new home in Seattle. Mr. Catt was as good as his word. He even arranged his affairs to concentrate his own business trips during his wife's spring and fall speaking trips. Thus it was as Mrs. Carrie Chapman Catt that the former Iowa farm girl took over the top post in the American woman suffrage movement.

Like Miss Anthony herself, many of the most devoted suffrage supporters were elderly women. Mrs. Elizabeth Cady Stanton, who had launched the movement in 1848, had passed her eightieth birthday; Mrs. Lucy Stone had recently died. It was a rather quaint old-fashioned group that Mrs. Catt found herself leading.

Mrs. Catt's own faith in the cause never wavered, but she felt almost relieved when the state of her husband's health made it necessary for her to resign in a few years. While she was in retirement, woman suffrage burst onto the nation's front pages.

In state after state, young women began flocking to join the suffrage ranks. Suffrage parades began marching down main streets in many cities. Rich women and factory women joined the cause. What the revived suffrage movement desperately needed was a leader—and so Mrs. Carrie Chapman Catt was drafted. In 1916, at the age of fifty-seven, she became commander of one of the most unusual campaigns the world has ever seen.

She immediately grasped the situation confronting her. Because of a variety of new developments in American life, pressure for woman suffrage had suddenly seemed to increase. But actually, a series of gradual changes had brought about a different climate. More women were getting a good education, more women were working outside the home, more women had the leisure to concern themselves with community problems. And to all of them, it seemed grossly unfair that women had no voice in their government.

Suffragettes preparing for a parade.

Yet powerful enemies stood in the way of the suffrage movement. It was then common for husbands and fathers to say firmly: "Woman's place is in the home!" The mere idea that their wives or daughters might think of marching in a suffrage parade provoked angry outbursts from many men. Newspaper writers ridiculed the suffrage leaders, calling them unwomanly and freakish.

Besides the opposition from numerous men—and some women—who felt on general principles that there was no need to change established ways, even stronger opposition came from other quarters. Organized political parties wanted no part of the reform, fearing their power would be threatened. Many churchmen opposed suffrage vehemently, on the grounds that the Bible itself forbade women to speak up; respected ministers claimed the Ameri-

can family would fall apart if wives could defy their husbands' views in the polling booth. Powerful business interests were also ready to fight woman suffrage, on the grounds that women might well vote for new laws checking their power. In addition, there was a belief, held by some women as well as men, that woman's nature was too delicate to permit participation in the rough-and-tumble atmosphere of American politics.

Mrs. Catt sometimes poked fun at her opponents. Once she told a Boston suffrage meeting that a recent setback had really been a good omen. Back when witches were being hunted in Salem, she said, the president of Harvard had signed a statement approving the practice. And a later president of the same institution had endorsed the Fugitive Slave Law. She went on:

"So when a petition against suffrage

130

for women is sent to the Massachusetts Legislature, we need not be surprised—and certainly not discouraged—because we find among the signers the president of Harvard College!"

Her pointed comment was "the hit of the evening," a Boston newspaper reported.

But usually, Mrs. Catt disposed more briskly of antisuffrage arguments. Leading her suffrage army into battle, she warned all enemies: "There is one thing mightier than kings or armies, congresses or political parties—the power of an idea when its time has come to move. The idea will not perish; the party which opposes it may."

Then Mrs. Catt proceeded to organize large forces of women in almost every state, until she had a political machine the likes of which the nation had not yet known. Fifty thousand banner-carrying suffragettes marched down Fifth Avenue in New York City. President Wilson in Washington was besieged by an endless stream of suffrage supporters, including some extremely militant young women who went so far as to chain themselves to the White House fence. Tactics such as this, which had upset England for the past several years, were frowned on by Mrs. Catt. As far as she was concerned, peaceful protest would carry the day.

So in state after state, she sent out teams of college girls and grandmothers to get suffrage petitions signed. Men in barber shops, men at baseball games, would look up to find a suffragette carrying a long sheet of paper. "Please sign, sir," came the polite request. Then in state after state, special elections were held to consider amending the state con-

stitution to give women the vote.

When a sufficient number of states had acted to give Congress evidence that this issue could not be ignored, Mrs. Catt mustered her forces for a full-scale attack on the United States Constitution.

Two-thirds of the members of both houses of Congress would have to vote in favor of suffrage if an amendment to the Constitution was to be approved. Then, before the amendment could become the law of the land, the legislatures of three-fourths of the states would have to vote to accept the change.

After the entrance of the United States into World War I in 1917, Mrs. Catt did not let her own forces relax their efforts. The parades and petitions kept right on making front-page news. It seemed to the suffrage camp that as long as President Wilson had proclaimed the overseas struggle as a war "to make the world safe for democracy," it was important for American democracy to redeem itself in the eyes of the world by giving American women a full share in their own government.

To help convince Congress, Mrs. Catt picked carefully briefed volunteers to pay repeated visits to the offices of every Representative and Senator. The nation's capital had become accustomed to pleaders for special interests and the word "lobbyist" had acquired an unpleasant ring. But Mrs. Catt's ladies were lobbyists of a sort that Washington had not known before. They wore white gloves and frilly shirtwaists—but they spoke of hard political facts.

Women were already voting in many states, as a result of amendments in individual state constitutions, Mrs. Catt's ladies said; sooner or later, all women would be voting. And a man who did not support the amendment now, the suffrage lobbyists delicately pointed out, would not get many feminine votes later.

What they did not mention was the fact that Mrs. Catt had secretly given her forces a deadline. The year 1920 would be the hundredth anniversary of Susan Anthony's birth. Mrs. Catt thought it most fitting to honor Aunt Susan's mem- ory by making sure the women of the United States could cast ballots in the 1920 Presidential election.

The first time Mrs. Catt let out her secret came after a tense vote in the House of Representatives on January 10, 1918. Wives and daughters everywhere in the United States had been working hard to change their menfolk's minds, and the effort brought results that day. A Tennessee Representative who broke

Nearly 135 years after the Declaration of Independence, women finally won the right to vote. Mrs. Catt (left) and a friend cast their first ballots.

his arm refused to go into a hospital to have the bone set until he had voted for suffrage. An Illinois Republican left the hospital where he had been confined for six months to whisper his "Aye" for suffrage. A New Yorker left the bedside of his dying wife—keeping his promise to her, he said—to cast his ballot in favor of the suffrage amendment. When the final tally was announced, showing that exactly the required two-thirds had endorsed the amendment, a woman's voice rose from the packed visitors' galleries.

"Praise God from Whom all blessings flow," she sang, and hundreds of other voices—women's voices and men's voices—joined in the reverent hymn. It was a moment unmatched in American history.

Mrs. Catt then revealed the 1920 deadline to newspaper reporters. But victory was not yet assured.

The Senators still had to be convinced, and that took more than a year. Not until May of 1919 did suffrage win in the Senate.

Then followed sixteen more hectic months, while the legislatures of three-quarters of the states voted to ratify the proposed Nineteenth Amendment. At 8:00 on the morning of August 26, 1920, the telephone rang in Mrs. Catt's Washington headquarters. After answering it, she turned to her anxious aides.

"Tennessee ratified at four-thirty this morning," she said. Thus ended a battle that had lasted almost three-quarters of a century, ever since Mrs. Stanton had first opened it. There could be no doubt that the victory would have taken years longer except for the awesomely efficient leadership of Mrs. Carrie Chapman Catt.

When Mrs. Catt got off a train in New York the following afternoon, Governor Al Smith and an Army band were waiting to greet her. As an enormous bouquet of flowers was thrust into her arms, the band struck up an appropriate march —"Hail the Conquering Hero Comes!" The last woman-suffrage parade then swung into line.

Now, having won the vote for America's women, Mrs. Catt helped to organize the League of Women Voters—a political-education group for women—which she had founded even before the adoption of the Nineteenth Amendment. She assisted suffrage drives in other countries. She also devoted much time to work for world peace until her death in 1947.

Neither money nor glory was Carrie Chapman Catt's goal as she strove to help women everywhere to the dignity of full citizenship. By her determined leadership, battling powerful forces that preferred to keep things as they were, she demonstrated that there is more than one kind of battlefield on which courage can be shown.

JONAS SALK
Conqueror of Polio

In the summer of 1952 three boys were lined up by their father. One after another, each brother had his arm jabbed with a sterile needle. If the boys were brave about submitting to the shots, their father was even braver.

He was Dr. Jonas Salk—and he was trying out his new polio vaccine on his own sons. He thought he had found the means to conquer that dreadful killing and crippling disease, but he needed proof. Peter, age nine, Darrell, six, and Jonathan, three, would help provide that proof.

Dr. Salk's decision to test the vaccine on his own children, and to inject himself and his wife as well, had not been lightly taken. After long months of careful research, Dr. Salk was certain that the serum he had developed would prove both safe and effective; yet there is always danger in any such experiment.

"I had the courage of my convictions," he explained later. "I couldn't have done it unless I had been more critical of myself than others were of me. It was courage based on confidence, not daring, and it was confidence based on experience."

The experience went back many years. Born in New York City on October 28, 1914, Jonas Edward Salk was the son of a garment-factory worker and his wife. The family was far from rich, but Jonas had been blessed with a keen mind.

While growing up in the Bronx, Jonas was exceptionally neat and precise about his belongings and his schoolwork. His younger brothers, Herman and Lee, would drop their books and their clothing anywhere, but Jonas always arranged his things neatly.

Shy by nature, he was not standoffish. He often joined the neighborhood boys in the city version of softball—stickball, a game in which a broom handle was used as the bat and manhole covers as the bases. When an argument developed, as quite frequently happened, the others tended to call on Jonas as umpire. They knew he would not lose his temper over the question of whether a boy was safe or out. "To him," a friend later recalled, "it was just another problem to be solved."

But Jonas' main interest in this period was books. He read everything he could get his hands on; as might be expected, he got exceptionally good marks in school. Because of his high grades, he was admitted to Townsend Harris Hall, a New York City high school for outstanding students.

He showed no special interest in science there; his main studies were in the classics. Before his sixteenth birthday, he was ready for college. His family could not afford to pay for his higher education, but that proved no great problem. Like many another poor, bright boy in New York, he won a place in the freshman class at C.C.N.Y.—the College of the City of New York, where no tuition fees were charged and the only requirement for acceptance was a high scholastic average. In this institution, filled with sharp, hard-working boys all striving to better themselves, Jonas Salk excelled.

More important, he took a science course during his first year—and found his life's work. After that, he spent his summers working as a laboratory technician and studying on his own. By the time he graduated in 1934, he knew exactly what he wanted to do with his life. He would be a medical scientist, not just a doctor but a scientist in medicine.

After enrolling in the New York University medical school, he spent an extraordinary number of hours at laboratory work, so many hours that he attracted the attention of his professors. If he wanted to become a research scientist, one of them suggested, he would need a better background in basic science. So young Jonas Salk dropped out of medical school for a year to study chemistry intensively.

Experimenting on his own then, he demonstrated such a grasp of research technique that he won several fellowships, which helped to pay his way during the rest of his formal medical training. He had no problem with his routine medical studies; and attracting the special interest of another one of his professors, he even branched out into a research project concerning influenza viruses.

His professor was Dr. Thomas Francis Jr., the man who almost twenty years later was to sit in judgment on Salk's most important work. Besides gaining the attention of Dr. Francis, young Dr. Salk also made an impression on a girl he liked. Not long after finishing his medical training in 1939, he married Miss Donna Lindsay, a social worker. And he continued working with Dr. Francis, collaborating on laboratory research.

Why did he seek research fellowships instead of going into the more lucrative practice of medicine? he was asked.

"Why did Mozart compose music?" he replied.

For there was no confusion in Dr. Salk's mind. He had not become a doctor to make money. He was a scientist in medicine, having no choice but to follow his natural research bent.

When Dr. Francis went out to Ann Arbor to take charge of a medical department at the University of Michigan, Dr. Salk followed. It was 1942 and World War II was raging. But his own battlefield would be a quiet laboratory, where the enemy was disease. If a way could be found to protect American soldiers against influenza, then the terrible sort of epidemic that had killed thousands in the First World War might be averted.

Salk then began to give serious study to viruses, those small infectious parasites about a millionth of an inch in size; and to vaccines, those substances injected into the body to produce immunity to disease. The first step in producing a vaccine was to find something that could successfully fight a particular family of disease-causing viruses.

Knowing that the human body itself was capable of making such substances under certain circumstances, Drs. Salk and Francis experimented with the flu virus, killed chemically in the laboratory. They found that a vaccine of killed flu viruses stimulated a patient's own system to produce antibodies that protected against flu infection.

It was not nearly so simple a matter, of course, but by working along these lines, Dr. Salk was taking the path that led to the polio vaccine.

When the University of Pittsburgh expanded its virus research program in 1947, Dr. Salk became the director of its Virus Research Laboratory. He and his associates kept busy trying to perfect the influenza vaccine, which had been successfully used during the war. In 1948 they turned to polio research, a field then attracting much scientific attention.

In that year, the National Foundation for Infantile Paralysis decided that if polio was ever going to be conquered, all-out war on the disease would have to be declared. The foundation had been helping polio victims and sponsoring research since its creation in 1938 by President Franklin D. Roosevelt. It was headed by a dynamic former law partner of Roosevelt's named Basil O'Connor, a man adept at raising money and spending it for research.

O'Connor stated that the first phase of the war on polio must be a massive effort to classify the various types of the disease. Dr. Salk's laboratory and

Dr. Salk with monkeys in his lab.

three others—at the Universities of Kansas, Utah and Southern California— took on the assignment. Three years, $1,370,000 and 30,000 monkeys later (the monkeys were used for tests), O'Connor had his answer: there were three distinct types of polio, and any vaccine would have to prevent all three.

The first major breakthrough in polio vaccine research came in 1949, when Dr. John Enders of the Children's Medical Center in Boston evolved a simple method for growing the deadly polio virus in a test tube. Dr. Enders and his team won a Nobel Prize for their discovery.

Now all polio researchers had the tool they needed to make a vaccine. But a very big question remained. How was the tool to be used?

With others, Dr. Salk and his associates held that chemically killed polio viruses presented the best opportunity. This approach had scored a marked success in the influenza program. But some other medical researchers put their faith in what they called an attenuated vac-

137

cine—a vaccine in which the virus had been weakened but not killed.

In the judgment of Basil O'Connor's money-raising foundation, the strongest hope for a swift conquest of polio lay in supporting every interested, qualified researcher. Dr. Salk was among those who received grants, and funds poured into Pittsburgh; Dr. Salk's staff grew to include fifty trained researchers. They worked on the top three floors of the Pittsburgh Municipal Hospital for Contagious Diseases with test tubes, monkeys and their own intuition, building on both their own discoveries and those of other researchers.

This is how they worked: they grew the three different kinds of polio virus in their test tubes, then killed the viruses by mixing them with formaldehyde, a disinfectant. The result was a vaccine of killed viruses. By injecting this into live monkeys, Salk and his associates proved that the monkeys developed antibodies which protected them against polio.

Thus described, the process may sound easy and logical. But it took Salk two years of methodical hard work, sometimes eighteen hours a day, seven days a week, to arrive at the formula he wanted. Since he was going against some strong medical opinion, it also took great courage for him to forge onward undiscouraged.

His own description of what he did was more down-to-earth. In his own words, the polio research was something like the performance of a housewife concocting a new kind of cake.

"She starts with an idea and certain ingredients," he said, "and then experiments, a little more of this, a little less

of that, and keeps changing things until finally she has a good recipe."

When Dr. Salk had his polio-preventing "recipe," he faced an enormous challenge. His vaccine worked on monkeys. But would it work on human beings?

Before he could find out, he had to be positive the vaccine was completely safe. He had to check against all conceivable harmful effects. With the same neat and precise care he had taken with his homework as a boy, he patiently made one preliminary test after another.

On June 30, 1952, Dr. Salk was ready for the first major test. The first human beings to be inoculated with his vacine were children who had had polio already and were immune to at least one type of polio; they were patients in the D. T. Watson Home for Crippled Children in nearby Lettsdale, Pennsylvania. His theory was that, if something went wrong, these children would not get polio again. But the test inoculations would still show whether or not the vaccine induced the human system to produce more polio antibodies.

Even though the danger involved was slight, Dr. Salk admitted to a friend: "When you inoculate children with a polio vaccine, you don't sleep well for two or three months."

But this first test was an unqualified success. No youngsters developed new symptoms, and their antibody levels rose. More experiments were made elsewhere. Then Dr. Salk proceeded with possibly his bravest experiment. Following a tradition in vaccine research, he gave test inoculations to his own family. These tests went off successfully, too.

138

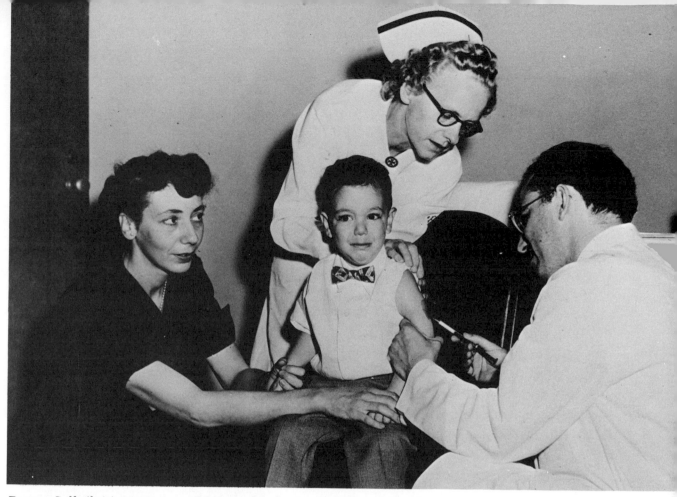

Donna Salk (left) appears confident as her husband injects their three-year-old son with trial polio vaccine.

By October of 1953, Dr. Salk was sure he had an effective polio vaccine. He was ready for a mass trial. One month later, Basil O'Connor announced that the large-scale test would begin as soon as sufficient supplies of the vaccine were available; and Dr. Francis agreed to set up the Poliomyelitis Vaccine Evaluation Center.

The unprecedented mass vaccinations started on April 26, 1954. Involved in the study were 1,829,916 children between the ages of six and nine. More than 20,000 doctors, 40,000 nurses, 50,-000 teachers and 200,000 adult volunteers took part in the experiment. No wonder science reporters said it was the greatest mass test of a medical discovery ever known.

With more than a hundred assistants,

Dr. Francis then set to work on his report. The excitement generated by the Salk vaccine was shown by the elaborate setting for the report's release. On the day it was due, one large auditorium at the University of Michigan in Ann Arbor looked more like a Hollywood movie set than a campus meeting hall. A battery of sixteen cameras, with shouting crews, focused on the stage from a specially built platform at the rear. In the corridors outside, curious students milled around more television cameras and radio microphones.

Inside the auditorium, there were no students. Their place for the day was taken by more than 150 reporters from all over the world, along with 500 doctors and medical scientists.

Had the vaccine worked? Had the

dreaded disease of polio been conquered? The careful, scientific answers to these questions were to be given in this hall within a few minutes.

The day was April 12, 1955, by coincidence the tenth anniversary of the death of Franklin D. Roosevelt, the man who had overcome the crippling disabilities of polio to become President of the United States. But thousands of others had been crippled worse, and thousands more had died of the disease.

At 10:20 A.M., Dr. Francis entered the auditorium. As spotlights blinked on and cameras whirred, he stepped behind a lectern decorated with the blue and gold seal of the University of Michigan.

Adjusting his horn-rimmed glasses, Dr. Francis began to read his report. It took him one hour and forty minutes to give the full scientific details—but to the world at large, only one basic fact mattered: the anti-polio vaccine developed by Dr. Salk was safe and effective!

If used properly, it could stamp out

Jonas Salk (right) conferring with Thomas Francis (left) and Basil O'Connor.

polio. One of the most fearful diseases known to man could now be prevented.

When the slender, scholarly Dr. Salk himself got up to speak, he was greeted by an ovation. But some doctors listened to him guardedly, as if they were not yet quite convinced.

For the mass test, exciting as the results seemed, still raised questions. While the detailed statistics left no doubt that the new vaccine was both safe and effective, the data did not show all that Dr. Salk had hoped; it indicated an effectiveness ranging between 60 and 90 per cent. In short, some people who received injections of the vaccine might still succumb to polio.

In his own report, Dr. Salk tried to reassure the doubters by describing the new procedures he had adopted since the start of the 1954 field test. By changing his method of producing vaccine, he had, he said, made it more powerful; its effectiveness would be greater. Furthermore, he went on, he could now recommend a new system of three injections in sequence as providing more positive protection. He ended by predicting that new tests might show 100 per cent protection of those vaccinated.

Then, despite some lingering reservations, a board of scientists present in Ann Arbor endorsed the Salk procedure. That same day the Secretary of Health, Education and Welfare, Mrs. Oveta Culp Hobby, approved the large-scale manufacture of the vaccine. She said: "It's a great day. It's a wonderful day for the whole world. It's a history-making day."

And her comments were echoed by newspapers everywhere. Church bells rang in some villages; prayers were offered in churches and synagogues; one Congressman proposed that Dr. Salk be granted a pension of $10,000 a year for life.

Meanwhile, drug companies hurriedly announced plans to manufacture vast quantities of the new vaccine. Thousands of cities and towns planned mass vaccination programs. No matter that some doctors were irritated by what they considered an unscientific emotional reaction—Dr. Jonas Salk was overnight a national hero, the man who had conquered polio.

Suddenly, a few weeks later, an emergency arose. Several cases of polio were reported among children who had only recently received injections, and the program was temporarily halted. In laboratories and at medical conferences, there were frantic efforts to find the trouble.

Throughout the crisis, Dr. Salk remained calm in public; privately, at medical meetings, he fought to defend his vaccine against those whose earlier doubts had been reinforced. Confronted with panic and hostility, Dr. Salk showed great courage as he kept claiming that his vaccine formula was sound—what the world has come to call moral courage. Holding to an idea when you are convinced of its rightness, even if many others dispute it, requires bravery of this nature, and Jonas Salk proved he had this quality in full measure.

Within a few months, Dr. Salk was once more vindicated. It was discovered that the haste with which the new vaccine had been produced had led to carelessness in a drug-manufacturing plant—and

new safeguards were adopted. The mass vaccinations resumed.

Ten years later, on April 12, 1965, Dr. Jonas Salk was summoned to the White House. President Lyndon B. Johnson congratulated him and then the Surgeon General of the United States, Dr. Luther Terry, reported that during the previous year there had been only 121 cases of polio in the entire country. During the worst year before the vaccine became available, 1952, there had been almost 58,000 new polio cases.

"This represents an historic triumph of preventive medicine," said the Surgeon General.

In reply, Dr. Salk, who had left Pittsburgh to become director of the Salk Institute of Biological Science at La Jolla, California, looked ahead to new challenges. He spoke of the continued need for research, striving toward discovery of the cure for such diseases as cancer.

Despite all the recognition he received, Dr. Salk himself remained a somewhat controversial figure. Within the medical profession, there still were some who minimized his contribution, particularly in the light of later events. Several years after Dr. Salk's dramatic success, Dr. Albert B. Sabin developed an attenuated vaccine, simpler to administer than the original. Instead of enduring unpleasant shots, millions of children now are protected from polio merely by eating a sugar cube treated with a few drops of Sabin vaccine.

Yet in the eyes of the world at large, to countless parents and children in almost every land, Dr. Jonas Salk is still a hero—the man who first triumphed over polio.

ALAN SHEPARD
First American Into Space

Alan Shepard awoke shortly after midnight. From the window of his room in Hangar S, he studied the sky. It sparkled with stars; not a cloud showed. Reassured, he went back to sleep.

An hour later he woke again, checked the time on his watch, swung his long legs out of bed. Within a few minutes, he was sitting down to a meal of orange juice, two poached eggs and a steak.

"It's really a tough life, having steak for breakfast," he remarked.

Thus started May 5, 1961, for Alan Bartlett Shepard Jr., formerly of East Derry, New Hampshire. As a boy, he had spent hour after hour tinkering with model airplanes. As a young officer fresh out of the United States Naval Academy, he had volunteered to be a test pilot. Now at the age of thirty-seven, he was about to undertake the crucial mission of his career—and one of the most daring explorations in all recorded history. He was going to be the first American to travel into outer space, the first to venture beyond the familiar and comfortable protection of the earth's atmosphere.

Only a little more than two years earlier, he and six other skilled pilots had been invited after vigorous screening to join a historic program. The United States was mounting a massive effort to explore outer space.

A new word had been coined to describe Shepard and his six companions—astronauts. And a new base had been built to house them—an enormously complex aerospace center on the sandy point of Florida then known as Cape Canaveral. (After President Kennedy's death, it was renamed Cape Kennedy.)

A training program was devised for the astronauts. Nobody really knew how the human body would react in the unexplored environment of outer space. Scientists and engineers could only make assumptions on the basis of the best scientific data available—and hope that the astronauts' training program was sufficient preparation for the spectacular adventure ahead.

The first seven astronauts studied astronomy, meteorology, biology, cramming in more scientific facts than most people learn in a lifetime. They were also dunked in ice water and baked in hot boxes heated to 135 degrees, to accustom their bodies to sharp temperature changes. They whirled in centrifuges to simulate the sense of weightlessness they would encounter aloft. They

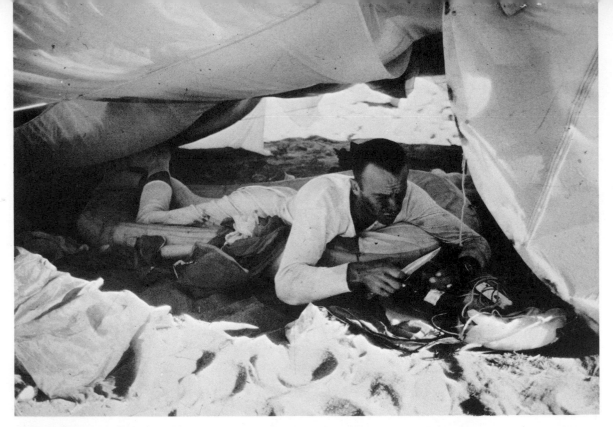

Survival in the desert was part of the astronauts' rigorous training. Here Alan Shepard, using his parachute as a tent, carves a pair of sandals.

walked on treadmills. They sat for hours in soundproof and totally dark chambers to harden themselves to such unnatural conditions. At least forty times each, they "took off" on the ground in simulated flights.

Then after twenty-four months, an actual flight was scheduled. Among the seven astronauts, Alan Shepard won the awesome assignment to the first flight.

It was still dark when Shepard finished his breakfast on that historic May 5, and above the silhouettes of giant cranes and towers the stars still sparkled. With the promise of fine weather, technicians at the launching site methodically carried on their preflight checking. And Shepard started on his own preparations, at the base medical headquarters.

Entering the building, he might have been any poster artist's picture of a handsome airman, tall and lanky, with blue eyes, a brown crew cut and an all-American grin. Fortunately he had stopped growing at just under six feet; for this particular mission the pilot's compartment was so cramped that six-footers were disqualified. Shepard was the tallest of the seven astronauts, and he had barely missed being turned away as oversized two years earlier.

Now he was not only weighed and measured and given a thorough physical check by the medics, he was also wired almost like a robot. Four small electronic devices to keep track of his heart's activity were pasted to his chest; a respirometer to measure his breathing was taped on; other medical measuring devices that would transmit precise data on his physical condition were set in place.

Once all of this had been done, Shepard set about putting on his space suit. Made of nylon, rubberized on the inside and aluminized on the outside, it gave the silvery impression of a costume some comic-strip hero might have worn. When he donned his space helmet, too, the impression was even more striking. Garbed thus, he strode out of the medical office at five minutes past four in the morning; the sky was still dark.

A large white van was waiting to take him to the launching pad. Shepard clambered aboard.

Climbing out at the launching site, Shepard had a portable air-conditioning unit in his hands. That only added to the almost eerie futuristic atmosphere, with clouds of liquid oxygen billowing out of the vents of the Redstone rocket that was gleaming in the glow of searchlights. Atop the tall thrusting rocket, sixty-five feet above the ground, perched a black, barrel-shaped Mercury capsule, with *Freedom 7* emblazoned on its side in white letters. Fellow astronauts stood by to greet Shepard and murmur private jokes to ease the tension he must be feeling. Boarding the elevator that would take him up to the capsule, Shepard grinned at John Glenn and Virgil "Gus" Grissom, two other members of the astronaut team.

"They really wanted to send a dog," Shepard said, "but they thought that would be too cruel."

For all of his outward calm, Shepard readily admitted later that he had been more than mildly keyed up when he reached the capsule, squeezed through the hatch and squirmed into position. "Okay, Buster," he recalled telling himself, "you volunteered for this thing. Now it's up to you to do it."

Despite the danger involved in daring the unknown, he had indeed volunteered, even though he was married and had two daughters to bring up. Laura was now fourteen and Juliana ten. The son of a retired Army colonel, Shepard had been born in East Derry, New Hampshire, on November 18, 1923, and almost immediately had started seeking out challenges. Exceptionally bright in school work, he made himself into a good athlete as well. A classmate at Annapolis remembered: "He amazed the coaches and everybody else, beating out bigger guys for a seat on the varsity rowing team."

Graduating from the Naval Academy near the end of World War II, Shepard had served on a destroyer, then had signed up for flight training. He was so impatient to get his wings that he even enrolled in a civilian flight school, too, during his spare time. After the war, he went into test piloting, flying high-altitude research missions.

In 1959 he was tapped as a possible astronaut. Project Mercury was to be the title of the first phase of the manned space-flight program under the auspices of the National Aeronautics and Space

Alan Shepard jokes with fellow astronauts and their doctor during his pre-flight breakfast, May 5, 1961.

Administration. This first phase, for which billions were being spent, aimed at putting one-man space capsules into orbit as preparation for sending men to the moon. Would he volunteer? The night Shepard received the letter asking the question, he solemnly consulted his wife.

"Why are you bothering to ask me?" she said, knowing her husband. "You know you'll do it anyway."

So here he was strapping himself into a cramped capsule, checking switches, inspecting dials. Suddenly a scrap of paper pasted to the instrument panel caught his eye. One of his colleagues was still trying to make him laugh. The little sign said: "No handball playing in this area."

The next several hours were agonizingly slow. Would the crucial test flight never start? Not only in the capsule and at Cape Canaveral, but everywhere in the world, the success—or failure—of this mission was a matter of intense interest.

Only a few weeks earlier, the Russians had scored a stunning triumph. Their cosmonaut Yuri Gagarin had been rocketed aloft to orbit the earth on April 12, 1961; he had opened a new space era by his spectacular feat.

The American space effort was not ready yet to match Gagarin's exploit. Only a brief sortie into space was planned for Shepard; there would be no orbiting for him. But a suborbital trip was still a dangerous, challenging adventure—and everyone would be watching. The Soviets had masked their probe in secrecy, merely announcing the successful outcome of Gagarin's flight after he landed, but the United States was taking a different tack. Newsmen from the world over were on hand to witness the Shepard launching, television cameras would whir, the whole world would see Alan Shepard's success—or failure. Shepard's own wife and two daughters would be watching on their television set. President Kennedy would be watching in the White House. In living rooms, in schools, outside store windows—wherever there was a television screen—millions of people would be watching to see what happened at Cape Canaveral.

The countdown proceeded, then stopped. There was a short delay because clouds had drifted over the launch site, but they blew off and the count resumed. Then it stopped again, because an electrical gadget began to overheat. After this trouble was solved, the count started and stopped once more, when pressure in a fuel line rose too high.

Over his capsule radio, Shepard spoke impatiently to technicians on the ground. "Why don't you fix your little problem and light this candle?" he asked.

The line was fixed, the countdown resumed again and this time no further hitch developed. The final seconds arrived.

"Ten . . .

"Nine . . .

"Eight . . ."

Then seven . . . six . . . five . . . four . . . three . . . two . . . one . . . zero . . .

"LIFT OFF!"

It was 9:34 A.M., Eastern Standard Time. From the capsule's radio came the calm voice of Alan Shepard: "Roger, lift off and the clock is started."

146

The last picture of Shepard before the capsule was sealed.

Then the Redstone rocket rose, seemingly slowly, a diamond-bright flame spurting from its tail. It climbed, picking up speed; for a moment it was lost behind a large cumulus cloud, then it reappeared, leaving a thin white trail against the blue sky.

In the capsule, being sped aloft, Shepard noted less vibration and noise than he had expected. After so many trial runs, the real experience seemed almost routine to him. His speed reached 5,180 miles an hour. "All systems are go," he reported.

Two minutes and twenty-two seconds after the flight started, the rocket engine cut off, at an altitude of 180,000 feet. The rocket separated from the capsule and fell away. Shepard switched over to manual control. Each time he moved his control stick, a tiny jet of hydrogen peroxide emerged from a nozzle outside the capsule, altering the capsule's direction. The system worked perfectly.

Having reported this to the ground, Shepard took time to look through his periscope at the earth.

"What a beautiful sight!" he exclaimed.

"I'll bet it is," said a voice from the ground.

While he marveled at his view of blue ocean and the Florida coast, and then tested one system after another, Shepard was experiencing the strange phenomenon of weightlessness. Except in experiments on the ground, no other man besides Yuri Gagarin had ever undergone this state. How did Shepard find it? Pleasant and relaxing, he reported.

After five minutes and eleven seconds, he reached the highest point of his trip—116.5 miles up. He had attained the mission's objective. Now it was time to come down.

Using his manual controls, Shepard tipped the blunt end of the capsule forward. Then the retro-rockets fired.

147

Suddenly he was pushed back into his seat, subjected to a force of about 11 g's, or eleven times the ordinary pull of gravity on earth. All at once it was as if he weighed 1,700 pounds, instead of his normal 160.

As he plunged toward earth, Shepard kept grunting over and over again: "Okay . . . okay . . . okay . . ." This was to let the anxious monitors on the ground know that he was still conscious and all was well. And it was. Although the temperature of the outside of the capsule built up to 1,230 degrees as it hurtled downward, inside the temperature did not rise above 100 degrees. Gradually the capsule slowed. At 30,000 feet, its speed was down to 300 miles an hour. The major danger of the flight —re-entry into the earth's atmosphere— had passed. But Shepard still had to land safely.

At 10,000 feet, the capsule's main parachute automatically opened. In a few seconds, Shepard reported: "I'm at seven thousand feet . . . my condition is good." At 9:49, fifteen minutes after the flight had started, Alan Shepard and his capsule landed in the Atlantic. He had rocketed into space only briefly, but it was enough. He had triumphantly demonstrated America's space-flight capability.

His landing took place right in the middle of the target area, 302 miles from the launching pad. A helicopter hovered overhead, and Shepard opened the capsule door. He crawled out and grabbed a sling let down by the copter. Seven minutes later, he stepped out onto the flight deck of the aircraft carrier *Lake Champlain* to the excited cheers of hundreds of sailors, and he stood, grinning, waiting for his capsule to be unloaded too. "I wanted to take one more look at *Freedom 7,*" he explained later. "I was pretty proud of the job it had done."

For the next two days, Shepard was put through extensive tests by doctors, but they did allow him time off to take a telephone call from Washington. It was President Kennedy, personally relaying his congratulations. "Thank you very much, Mr. President," said Shepard. "It certainly was a very thrilling ride."

As for his medical testing, Shepard assured the doctors he had come through in fine shape. "I don't think there's much you'll have to do to me," he told them. And when all the testing was finished, they agreed completely with his verdict; he was in excellent physical condition. So they released him for an experience possibly almost as awesome as the flight itself.

At Cape Canaveral and then in Washington, D.C., Alan Shepard was treated to a hero's welcome. There were parades, press conferences, a gigantic outpouring of enthusiasm which the astronaut endured with patient good humor. He even won more plaudits for the way he bore himself through all the excitement. In *The New York Times* James Reston wrote:

"Commander Alan Shepard had a triumph in Washington today because he revived the faith of a sad and disillusioned city.

"It was not that he represented the courage of this country's first explorer of outer space—everybody expected that —or because he was something new. On the contrary, it was because he symbolized what Washington was created to celebrate but had begun to doubt: the free and natural man, simple, direct, thoughtful and modestly confident."

Alan Shepard—like Yuri Gagarin—had proved that man could survive in the hostile environment of outer space and perform his duties there without too much trouble. After him would come John Glenn, the first American to orbit the earth, and other astronauts who performed other tasks in space. But when the histories of man's steps to the moon and the stars are written, no matter how many centuries from now, the name of Alan Shepard, the first American to take the necessary first step into space, will lead the rest.

A helicopter lifts Shepard from Freedom 7 *(lower left).*

ERNIE PYLE

"Here Is Your War"

As a boy, he rode down a dusty Indiana dirt path to school on the back of a bony horse. It was that horse—the horse he rode to school and also followed behind a plow—that made Ernie Pyle decide against farming as his life's work.

"I decided that anything was better than looking at the south end of a horse going north," he explained much later.

Born on August 3, 1900, he had been raised on a small farm outside of Dana, Indiana. He seemed destined to become a farmer, as his father and his grandfather before him had.

But Ernie was different from the normal run of farm boys, mainly because he was timid. At lunchtime he never played in the usual schoolyard games, preferring to sit under a tree, munching an apple. When he went off to the University of Indiana, he still had no clear idea of what he wanted to do, except that farming was out.

He felt no great urge to write, but turned to journalism because he thought it was the easiest course available. He worked on the *Indiana Daily Student,* but frequently went for long walks all by himself. When the other journalism students gathered at the campus candy kitchen to hear a classmate, Hoagy Car-

michael, play the piano, Pyle sat off in a corner. Smiling and affable, he listened quietly, alone as usual.

If any one thing inspired him during this period, it was a story written in 1921 by Kirke Simpson of the Associated Press. The story described in simple, moving terms the burial of the Unknown Soldier in Arlington Cemetery. Simpson won the Pulitzer Prize for his story; it moved Ernie Pyle to tears and gave him a goal for the first time in his life. He wanted to write like that.

Just before graduation, he became a reporter for an Indiana paper, the *La Porte Herald;* he later moved on to newspapers in Washington and New York. The timid young man found, as had many shy people, that sensitivity and writing skill make better reporters than brashness and conviviality. In the days when aviation was booming, he became an aviation writer and grew with the industry. In 1932 he became managing editor of the *Washington News.*

Three years later, tense and ill, he went off to Arizona to recuperate. On his return, he wrote several columns about his vacation, trivial in content but interesting to read—and a new career was born. He became a roving correspondent for the Scripps-Howard newspapers. With his wife, Geraldine, he started to travel and to write.

Each day's experiences provided material for a column—a simple, chatty letter aimed at those who could never make the same trip. He wrote about the drought in North Dakota and how it affected the lives of the farmers there. He visited the Dionne quintuplets. He went to a leper colony and to Devil's Island. He traveled by train, boat, plane, horse and mule; he crossed the United States thirty-five times; he wore out three typewriters and three cars.

When the war broke out in Europe in September of 1939, "a small voice came in the night and said go." Ernie Pyle was off to London and a new phase of his career.

Only five feet eight, weighing about 110 pounds, he looked neither like a dashing war correspondent nor like a hero. He habitually wore a faded pair of Army chinos and an olive-drab wool cap that gave him a somewhat gnomish air. What was left of his red hair had by then turned grey.

Still a shy man, Pyle wandered around the battle areas, forcing himself to talk to soldiers. He liked people, but was tortured by the idea of striking up conversations. "I suffer agony in anticipation of meeting anybody, for fear they won't like me," he once explained. "Once I'm past the meeting I'm all right."

He was more than all right. It may have been surprising to him, but Ernie Pyle quickly became one of the most popular men wherever he went. Soldiers, sailors, marines, unlettered men and the educated alike, privates to generals—all were drawn to this shy, frail man from the Midwest. They shared their food, their shelter and their thoughts with him. Perhaps it was because he was a good listener; perhaps because he came and lived with them when he could have remained safe at the rear. But had he stayed safely back from the fighting, he never could have written as he wrote one day from Italy:

In this war I have known a lot of officers who were loved and respected by the soldiers under them. But never have I crossed the trail of any man as beloved as Captain Henry T. Waskow, of Belton, Texas.

Captain Waskow was a company commander in the Thirty-sixth Division. He had led his company since long before it left the States. He was very young, only in his middle twenties, but he carried in him a sincerity and a gentleness that made people want to be guided by him.

"After my father, he came next," a sergeant told me.

"He always looked after us," a soldier said. "He'd go to bat for us every time."

"I've never known him to do anything unfair," another said.

I was at the foot of the mule trail the night they brought Captain Waskow down. The moon was nearly full, and you could see far up the trail, and even partway across the valley below.

Dead men had been coming down the mountain all evening, lashed onto the backs of mules. They came lying belly-down across the wooden pack-saddles, their heads hanging down on one side, their stiffened legs sticking out awkwardly from the other, bobbing up and down as the mules walked.

The Italian mule skinners were afraid to walk beside dead men, so Americans had to lead the mules down that night. Even the Americans were reluctant to unlash and lift off the bodies when they got to the bottom, so an officer had to do it himself and ask others to help.

I don't know who that first one was. You feel small in the presence of dead men, and you don't ask silly questions.

They slid him down from the mule, and stood him on his feet for a moment. In the half-light he might have been merely a sick man standing there leaning on the others. Then they laid him on the ground in the shadow of the stone wall alongside the road. We left him there beside the road, that first one, and we all went back into the cowshed and sat on water cans or lay on the straw, waiting for the next batch of mules.

Somebody said the dead soldier had been dead for four days, and then nobody said anything more about it. We talked soldier talk for an hour or more; the dead man lay all alone, outside in the shadow of the wall.

Then a soldier came into the cowshed and said there were some more bodies outside. We went out into the road. Four mules stood there in the moonlight, in the road where the trail came down off the mountain. The soldiers who led them stood there waiting.

"This one is Captain Waskow," one of them said quietly.

Two men unlashed his body from the mule and lifted it off and laid it in the shadow beside the stone wall. Other men took the other bodies off.

Ernie was a favorite with the fighting men overseas.

Finally, there were five lying end to end in a long row. You don't cover up dead men in the combat zones. They just lie there in the shadows until somebody comes after them.

The unburdened mules moved off to their olive grove. The men in the road seemed reluctant to leave. They stood around, and gradually I could sense them moving, one by one, close to Captain Waskow's body. Not so much to look, I think, as to say something in finality to him and to themselves. I stood close by and I could hear.

One soldier came and looked down, and he said out loud, "God damn it!"

That's all he said, and then he walked away.

Another one came, and he said, "God damn it to hell anyway!" He

153

looked down for a few last moments and then turned and left.

Another man came. I think he was an officer. It was hard to tell officers from men in the dim light, for everybody was bearded and grimy. The man looked down into the dead captain's face and then spoke directly to him, as though he were alive, "I'm sorry, old man."

Then a soldier came and stood beside the officer and bent over, and he too spoke to his dead captain, not in a whisper but awfully tenderly, and he said, "I sure am sorry, sir."

Then the first man squatted down, and he reached down and took the captain's hand, and he sat there for a full five minutes holding the dead hand in his own and looking intently into the dead face. And he never uttered a sound all the time he sat there.

Finally he put the hand down. He reached over and gently straightened the points of the captain's shirt collar, and then he sort of rearranged the tattered edges of the uniform around the wound, and then he got up and walked away down the road in the moonlight, all alone.

The rest of us went back into the cowshed, leaving the five dead men lying in a line end to end in the shadow of the low stone wall. We lay down on the straw in the cowshed, and pretty soon we were all asleep.

This kind of writing made Ernie Pyle the best known and best loved of all the war correspondents in World War II.

Most correspondents came up to the front lines during the day to gather their material. They returned to the rear at night to write and send off their stories.

Ernie cheers wounded soldiers outside their hospital tent.

But Pyle operated differently. He came to the front lines to stay, perhaps ten days at a time. He knew the men he lived with; he listened attentively, taking no notes except names and addresses. Then he would go back and write until he had exhausted his material.

Many other correspondents wrote about the grand strategy, about armies advancing and retreating, about the politicians and the generals; but not Ernie Pyle. He told the story of GI Joe, the individual American fighting man.

For the fighting infantryman, there was no rest. And Ernie Pyle felt that he, too, had an obligation to return to the fighting front. His job was to convey to the American public a feeling of what it was like up there with the "mud-rain-frost-and-wind boys"—the foot soldiers who faced the enemy day after day after day. During the African campaign, he had written:

154

For four days and nights they had fought hard, eaten little, washed none and slept hardly at all. Their nights had been violent with attack, fright, butchery, their days sleepless and miserable with the crash of artillery.

The men were walking. They were fifty feet apart for dispersal. Their walk was slow, for they were dead weary, as a person could tell even when looking at them from behind. Every line and sag of their bodies spoke of their inhuman exhaustion. . . .

They didn't slouch. It was the terrible deliberation of each step that spelled out their appalling tiredness. Their faces were black and unshaved. They were young men, but the grime and whiskers and exhaustion made them look middle-aged. In their eyes as they passed was no hatred, no excitement, no despair, no tonic of their victory—there was just the simple expression of being there as if they had been there doing that forever, and nothing else.

Thus Ernie Pyle described the war and the men in it—and his columns were eagerly awaited throughout the United States. Millions read his reports; some of them were mailed back to the fighting fronts so that the soldiers themselves could read about what was happening elsewhere.

Like a soldier himself, Ernie Pyle kept on going—to the invasion of Sicily, the landings in Italy, to the Anzio beachhead. As long as the war was not over, his job was not complete.

When the press headquarters on the Anzio beachhead was bombed, Pyle reported:

Among the ruins of a shell-shattered French village, Ernie talks to a survivor.

I was astonished at feeling no pain, for debris went tearing around every inch of the room, and I couldn't believe that I hadn't been hit. But the only wound I got was a tiny cut on my right cheek from flying glass, and I didn't even know when that happened. The first I knew of it was when blood ran down my chin and dropped onto my hand.

Pyle walked out of the bombed-out building; the other correspondents, who had given him up for lost, began to call their 43-year-old colleague "Old Indestructible."

After Italy, Pyle landed in France the day after D-Day, June 6, 1944, when Allied troops stormed ashore and began the direct attack on Nazi-held Europe. His reaction was muted and caught the hearts of his countrymen:

155

Ernie relaxing with his wife Geraldine at their home in New Mexico.

I took a walk along the historic coast of Normandy in the country of France. It was a lovely day for strolling along the seashore. Men were sleeping in the sand, some of them sleeping forever. Men were floating in the water, but they didn't know they were in the water, for they were dead.

Pyle was almost killed by bombs from our own planes as they blasted a path for the breakout from St. Lo in Normandy, but he stayed with the infantry during the Battle of France. Day after day, he wrote home about men being killed alongside him, until he had enough. But after Paris was captured in August, Pyle wrote that he was coming home.

I've had it, as they say in the Army. I have had all I can take for a while.

I have been twenty-nine months overseas since the war started, have written about 700,000 words about it; have totalled nearly a year in the front lines . . . my spirit is wobbly and my mind is confused. The hurt has finally become too great.

And so Ernie Pyle, who thought he would collapse if he saw another dead man or if he had to write another column, returned home. He and his wife went back to a new home in Albuquerque. The infantrymen that he loved understood; so did his readers.

But Pyle himself was desperately unhappy. For hours he stared across the lonely and peaceful New Mexico mesa, brooding. There was a war going on in the Pacific, and he was standing aside. He was afraid and he knew it; he had a premonition that he could not go on forever. But he knew that he had to go. He would have shaken his head in embarrassed dismay had anyone told him he was acting like a hero. In his own words:

"I'm going simply because there's a war on and I am part of it, and I've known all along that I was going back. I'm going simply because I've got to— and I hate it."

By February of 1945, Pyle had flown to the Marianas at the doorstep of Japan. He wrote then about the men who flew the B-29s that bombed Japan; he landed with the Marines on Okinawa; and then he went on to the nearby island of Ie Shima to observe the fighting there.

On the morning of April 18, with a lieutenant colonel and some others, he drove forward in a jeep to get nearer to the fighting. A Japanese machine gun suddenly opened fire. Pyle and the others leaped out into a ditch. A moment later, Pyle raised his head to look around. Another burst of machine-gun fire sprayed the ground. Pyle was killed instantly.

The word of Ernie Pyle's death spread around the world. President Truman, generals and soldiers everywhere mourned. Of all the correspondents who covered the war, Ernie Pyle had best described the reality of war. He had put the horror in simple, human terms that touched his readers more than any casualty statistics could, and by doing so had served American democracy well. By his unassuming dedication, he had won the love of his countrymen.

He had, in addition, won numerous prizes and awards, among them the Pulitzer Prize for distinguished journalism, just as he had dreamed back at the University of Indiana. But the tribute that surely would have meant the most to him was the simple monument placed over the spot where he was killed:

AT THIS SPOT

THE

77TH INFANTRY DIVISION

LOST A BUDDY

ERNIE PYLE

18 APRIL 1945

MARIAN ANDERSON
Voice of Glory

The oldest of the three Anderson sisters was well known to all the neighbors. Since the age of six, Marian had been singing every Sunday in the choir of the Union Baptist Church. When she had a solo part, the pastor and the whole congregation would listen in positive awe.

To hear her sing even an old familiar hymn could bring tears of pure joy. Some said the sound of her voice gave the feeling of the richest velvet. As for Marian herself, she only knew she never felt so cozy and happy as she did singing.

In other ways she shared the common lot, for her family was no different from most in South Philadelphia, where she was born. Every so often, her father managed to get odd jobs to add to what he earned by delivering coal or ice, and her mother sometimes went to work in other people's houses doing their laundry, leaving the girls with their grandmother. Still, the Andersons always had to count their money carefully by the penny.

It rarely struck Marian that they were poor, though. Up and down the block, nobody was much better off. Unlike some others, the Andersons never went hungry, and once a year they had the splendid treat of taking a trolley ride clear across town to see the circus. Just one thing disturbed Marian. If only she had had the money, she would have dearly loved to take music lessons.

From the age of eight, she worked after school to make money—first for penny candy and later for music lessons. Her first job was scrubbing front steps on the street where she lived. For cleaning a neighbor's steps till they gleamed, she could earn as much as five cents.

But before she collected enough to start lessons, everything changed for the Andersons. Her father was hurt so badly in an accident that he could no longer work; when she was twelve, he died. Then the need for money was so serious that it seemed Marian might have to quit school and help her mother provide food for the younger girls, Alyce and Ethel.

Such a solution would never satisfy Mrs. Anderson. She had taught a country school in Virginia in her younger days, before moving up to Philadelphia. Without sufficient training to teach in the city schools, she hadn't been able to spare time since coming north to improve her own education; but she was determined that her daughters must do better. Marian must go to high school, she said firmly.

In later years, Marian returned to visit her old schoolroom in Philadelphia.

And the pastor and the congregation of their church agreed. So deeply had Marian's music moved them that they wanted to show their appreciation; and possibly there were some already thinking that a voice like this girl's had to be heard beyond their own neighborhood. Thus one Sunday morning, after the regular collection for church purposes had been taken, the pastor rose and said solemnly:

"We want to do something for our Marian."

Once again the ushers passed out collection baskets. Hand after hand reached into pocket or purse to draw out a hard-earned coin that could not easily be spared.

Marian Anderson never forgot the exact total of the pennies, nickels and dimes her good neighbors contributed to her that Sunday: it was $17.02.

With it, Mrs. Anderson and Marian went shopping. Shoes were what Marian needed most. Then they bought a few lengths of satin and some gold braid in the five-and-dime store. When they sat down together to sew a party dress, Marian's large brown eyes were excited, but not with thoughts of parties. She was thinking of the songs she would sing, now that she would have a dress fit for wearing at concerts.

For already organizations in the neighborhood were inviting her to sing at their meetings. They also offered to pay her fifty cents or even a dollar, and the money would more than come in handy. Above all, the chance of meeting other singers, who might be able to tell her how to go about studying music, thrilled Marian.

When she was singing at all sorts of meetings in the area while going to high school, she did impress people who knew something of music. Her high-school principal was impressed, too, and recommended that she study music seriously at a special school. But Marian had to tell all such well-wishers that until she managed to save the money, any special schooling would have to wait.

Yet almost sooner than she had dared hope, she had enough in the bank for a start. An aunt with a head for business had insisted she begin charging five or even ten dollars to sing at large meetings, and the increased fees made her bank balance mount much faster than expected.

One September morning Marian rode downtown, feeling nervous. The thought that at last she was going to study music was so exciting that she wondered why her knees were not shaking when she walked into the office where she had been told to inquire. But already she had become accustomed to standing up to sing before strangers, and her nervousness did not show.

Tall for her age, she also had the poise of a grown woman. She was dressed neatly; her dark, waving hair had been brushed till it shone. But as she took her place in the line of applicants, she was startled by the odd look the woman at the front desk gave her.

One after another, those ahead of Marian stepped up to the desk and received application forms. When it was her turn, the woman at the desk looked right past her and spoke to the person next in line. This continued till nobody else was left in the line.

Then the woman finally spoke to Marian Anderson.

"What do *you* want?" she asked.

Marian had been trying for several minutes not to be upset by this strange procedure. She explained as simply as she could that she had come to inquire about enrolling in the school.

The woman eyed her coldly and said: "We don't take colored."

Too stunned to answer, Marian turned and silently started home. Ever since her earliest years, she had of course been aware that she and her family had dark skins, and that many other people had light skins. From time to time, she had gathered that life was not as easy for those with dark skins. But although the neighborhood where she grew up was predominantly Negro, some white families lived there, too, and she had always got on well with them. Now for the first time in her life, she faced the blunt fact that the mere color of her skin made some people reject her.

Instead of complaining, Marian made other plans. Not a pushing sort of person, she did not want to cause trouble. But she was not about to give up her plans for studying music, either. Somehow she would learn what she had to— and keep on singing.

Private music lessons would be the obvious answer, if she could afford them. Even with the general grounding that a music school would have provided, individual lessons still would have been necessary sooner or later. Now she simply made up her mind to work and work in order to pay for the training she needed.

During these hard years, there were many who helped her. Every few months, someone who had never before heard Marian Anderson sing would listen bemused and then burst into praise. But mainly it was from her own people that encouragement came.

While she was still in her teens, invitations to sing began arriving from Negro churches and then Negro colleges as far away as Alabama. The fees they could offer were not high; sometimes the money she made hardly paid her train fare. And traveling presented countless problems. By now she had an accompanist to play the piano while she sang, and he too was dark-skinned. On trains going south from Washington, they had to sit in the car directly behind the engine, always the dirtiest and least comfortable. Only in the curtained-off area of the diner where the waiters ate could they be served hot food. Only in private homes could they stay overnight, for no hotel would take them. Yet no matter what indignities she had to endure, Marian Anderson put up with them and did not complain. She thought that earning money to pay her singing teacher was more important.

The invitations from Negro institutions in many states were a big help, but her old neighborhood in South Philadelphia did not forget her. At a special program arranged to raise money for "our Marian," the community contributed more than $600.

By the time Marian Anderson was a young woman, it was abundantly clear, at least to her old neighbors, that she had been no mere child wonder. As she matured, her voice gained an added richness; it was a thrilling contralto with so remarkable a range that she could sing low notes and high notes, too, far beyond the capacity of ordinary contraltos.

Furthermore, she was learning singing technique now. "How do you produce low D?" her first teacher had asked her. Marian had not the faintest idea. She simply opened her mouth, and there the proper tone was. But day after day she was conscientiously practicing voice placement now, and breathing exercises. She was also learning to sing the songs of famous composers. Where once she had known only the hymns and spirituals that she'd heard her mother hum, she now practiced Schubert and Brahms.

These new favorites could never quite displace the old, though. Her heart filled with religious fervor every time she sang the simple melodies of her childhood. Above all others, one moved her most deeply. Standing before any audience, unaffectedly clasping her hands as if in prayer, she would send forth waves of reverent emotion as she sang:

> He's got the whole world in His hands
> He's got the wind and rain in His hands
> He's got the sun and moon right in His hands
> He's got the whole world in His hands . . .

Gradually, the audiences that came to hear her began to include some white faces. But important concert managers did not appear with contracts. As the young Miss Anderson was only too well aware herself, she still had much to learn, particularly foreign languages; singing songs written by German or French or Italian composers was most unsatisfactory when one did not know the meaning of the words. Nevertheless, the big barrier to success continued to be her color.

Several times, after trying in vain to break out of her dogged routine of singing only to the same audiences, she was tempted to quit. Yet by now she felt she could not make such a decision on her own. Too many of her people had put their faith in her; she owed it to them to forget slights and cold looks.

Instead of quitting, she took every penny she had saved and went to Europe.

It was during a visit to Scandinavia that Marian Anderson scored her first major triumph.

Staid Stockholm was so excited when she sang there that a newspaper writer said the whole city had come down with "Marian Fever." In Finland she was invited to pay a personal call on the great Sibelius, one of the most eminent composers alive. After the famed conductor Arturo Toscanini heard her, he brought tears to her eyes by remarking:

"A voice like yours is heard only once in a hundred years."

With European concert managers begging her to sing everywhere on the continent, it seemed logical to some people that Miss Anderson ought to stay overseas. Fame and financial success were

Marian with her European music teacher.

hers if she lived abroad; and there were few if any doors closed to her there because of the color of her skin.

But Marian Anderson had no such intention.

Far too self-effacing to say she was needed in her own country, still she knew what she had to do. She would have shaken her head in dismay if anybody told her she was acting like a heroine. Many years later, she explained her decision in these simple words:

"There were other people to be considered—all the friends and neighbors who had believed in me. They had not helped me and had faith in me to see me run away to Europe. I had gone to Europe to achieve something, to reach for a place as a serious artist, but I never doubted that I must return. I was—and am—an American."

And so she returned to her native land in 1935, to spend several decades quietly doing her best to open more doors for Negroes. By her dauntless courage over these years, she amply demonstrated true heroism of a high order.

Her first concert back in New York was an extraordinary personal triumph. On shipboard, during an Atlantic storm, she had slipped and broken an ankle, but she refused to consider postponing her appearance. Reports about her from Europe had aroused great interest in the musical world, and she wanted to make sure the interest did not evaporate while her ankle mended. On the other hand, she could not bear the thought that some might say she was appealing for sympathy by hobbling onto the stage with her foot in a plaster cast.

So she insisted on a change in ordinary

procedure. When a select audience filed into Town Hall on the evening of her appearance, the stage curtain was closed, not open as is usually the case in musical performances. Only when the concert was scheduled to begin was the curtain drawn, disclosing Miss Anderson already standing gracefully near the piano. Possibly the sharpest-eyed could note that she seemed to be leaning slightly on the piano for support; but nobody could see that beneath the folds of her evening dress one foot was encased in a cast.

Still it was not to see Miss Anderson, but to hear her, that the knowing among New York's music lovers had come to Town Hall that evening. They were well rewarded. One critic described her as "a contralto of stunning range and volume." According to another comment, "Miss Anderson has the transcending quality of all authentic art—a genuine emotional identification with the core of the music."

Thus, while still in her twenties, Marian Anderson won an unquestioned place in the top rank of musical artists.

Franz Rupp and Marian Anderson sharing a bow. He was her accompanist for more than twenty years.

But in the next thirty years, she won even more renown as a symbol for her people—and of her people.

Although she frequently and generously gave credit to all who helped her, it was her own spirit that inspired her career. That was proved in 1939, when an organization priding itself on its patriotism refused to allow her to sing from the stage of its concert hall in Washington, D.C.

Instead of denouncing the Daughters of the American Revolution for barring her because of her color, Marian Anderson reacted in her own way. "You lose a lot of time hating people," she said gently.

But this episode led to one of the most stirring moments in American history. On Easter Sunday that year, 75,000 Americans gathered in front of the Lincoln Memorial to hear the singer the D.A.R. had scorned. Government officials had organized the unprecedented outdoor concert to show the world that the ideals of the American Declaration of Independence still had meaning in the nation's capital, despite the rudeness of a small group of conservative ladies.

Thenceforth, wherever she went on concert trips in the United States and on almost every other continent, Marian Anderson was received as an unofficial ambassador. "She is the best diplomat the United States ever sent overseas," one foreign leader commented. Finally, in 1957, the State Department recognized that her concert tours had actually been serving her country's purposes, and sent her on an extensive good-will mission to the Far East.

By then she had sung before millions

of people. She had been the first of her race to be admitted into many hotels, and her gracious manner had made the way easier for many Negroes who came after her. She had been the first Negro to sing with the Metropolitan Opera Company; she had won countless honorary degrees and medals.

Everywhere she had lifted the hearts and the hopes of the dark-skinned. When colored mothers with a glow of pride on their faces brought their children to see her, she always had time to smile and encourage them. After she could afford to make life comfortable for her family, she never forgot her own hard times; and without any fanfare she helped many others who were in need.

At the same time, her simple dignity touched countless thousands. If some artists made themselves noted for fits of temper and high-flown bragging, Marian Anderson was just the opposite. She carried modesty to the point of hardly ever using the word "I" when she was interviewed. Asked about her tastes in food, she would merely smile and murmur: "When one is hungry, one eats."

Further evidence that Marian Anderson had made her mark as an outstanding American came from President Dwight D. Eisenhower. In 1958 he appointed her a member of the American delegation to the United Nations.

"She has always represented something that transcends singing and embraces humanity," *The New York Times* said on the occasion of the appointment. As she moved toward the close of her active singing career, Miss Anderson continued to make friends for America when she served on various United Nations

Miss Anderson takes a curtain call after her stunning debut at the Metropolitan Opera.

human-rights committees.

Now she gradually curtailed her concert appearances, spending more and more time gardening and cooking at her Connecticut farm. In 1943 she had married Orpheus Fisher, a New York architect; now for the first time she was able to devote many months a year to quiet housewifely pursuits.

She formally retired from the concert stage in 1965, but she was still called on to speak at public meetings. She retained the deep affection of millions of her fellow citizens no matter what the color of their skins; and she returned the compliment.

She ended *My Lord, What a Morning!,* the book she wrote about her life, with these words:

"I have a great belief in the future of my people and my country."

DWIGHT D. EISENHOWER
Soldier for Democracy

All of the Eisenhower boys loved to play tag on the roof of their father's barn. People driving buggies down South East Fourth Street in the thriving Kansas town of Abilene became quite accustomed to the sight of the six brothers chasing each other up near the very peak of the gable—but which boy was which?

In order of their ages, there were Arthur and Edgar and Dwight; then Roy, Earl and Milton. But because the sound of their last name so clearly suggested it, each boy as he got beyond the lowest grades came to be called "Ike." Usually there were two Eisenhowers in a particular school at one time, and so they were "Little Ike" and "Big Ike."

Not till Dwight crossed the railroad tracks to enter the seventh grade did he single himself out noticeably. He did it first with his fists.

Like many another small town of the time, Abilene was divided in more ways than one by the train tracks running through it. North of the tracks, houses were bigger and more comfortable; the so-called "best people" lived here. South of the tracks was much less fashionable, and the Eisenhowers lived just about as far south as it was possible to be without getting out into open farm country.

Practically every year, when a new crop of South Side boys was promoted into the North Side school where all of Abilene's seventh- and eighth-graders went, there was an unofficial championship fight. Dwight's brother Ed—Big Ike to the whole playground—had stood up for their part of town the preceding year and beaten the best the rich boys had to offer.

Little Ike—David Dwight Eisenhower on school records, Dwight David to his own family, an arrangement he liked better and later decided on—Little Ike thought he had to uphold Ed's record. He ended up setting a new record of his own.

The North Side challenger he faced was a boy named Wesley Merrifield, much bigger and heavier than most twelve-year-olds and known throughout the town as an outstanding athlete. On the other hand, Dwight was slender for his age and not particularly noted for strength or speed.

But Dwight would not give up. During the first few minutes of the struggle he took awful punishment; his eyes were almost shut by angry purple swellings and his lip was bleeding. Still he stayed on his feet. Soon the bigger boy tired,

167

and then the fight turned into an endurance contest.

For two whole hours, without any rest, the two boys kept right on doggedly lunging at each other, landing punches often enough to bruise each other almost beyond recognition. Finally, Merrifield called a halt.

"Ike," he gasped, "I can't lick you."

"Well, Wes," said Ike handsomely, "I *haven't* licked you."

It was three days till Ike's wounds healed to the point where he could go back to school, by which time he had become known as the hero of "the toughest kid fight" in Abilene's history. With his likable grin and sunny disposition (except when his fiery temper was roused), he soon became one of the most popular boys in town.

Why he had fought so hard was the sort of question he never asked himself. When a thing had to be done he did it, without bothering to brood over the reasons. Pressed to explain, he might have offered something about proving Eisenhowers were as good as anybody, but it certainly had not been envy that had spurred him in the schoolyard fight.

From his earliest years, Dwight had well understood that his family was not rich. Shortly before he was born, his father had failed as a storekeeper. To support the family somehow, Mr. Eisenhower had left Kansas to take the first job he could find, in a railroad repair shop, in the dusty town of Denison, Texas. There Dwight was born on October 14, 1890. Missing Abilene relatives and friends, Mr. and Mrs. Eisenhower moved back when Dwight was ten months old. Ever since, they had scraped along on what Mr. Eisenhower got for tending the machinery at a local dairy.

Yet Dwight never felt sorry for himself; none of the Eisenhower boys did. That was their mother's doing, for she brought them up to accept hard work as normal. Even before each boy was old enough for school, he had his share of chores. A week at a time, it would be his turn to get out of bed before five in the morning to bring in kindling and light the kitchen stove. When that task fell to another brother, there would be instead watering the horse, feeding the pigs and chickens, gathering the eggs.

Summers, Dwight spent long hours hoeing vegetables on the three-acre plot adjoining their house. Then he and Ed would drive the horse and buggy over to the North Side to try to make a little money by selling their surplus of corn and tomatoes.

But if Mrs. Eisenhower gave her boys jobs almost as soon as they could walk, and was quick to reach for a maple switch when any boy disappointed her, she also allowed them ample hours for pure play. No amount of noise or rough-and-tumble upset her—except when one sort of game was involved.

Being on the edge of the raw and exciting cowboy country, the boys naturally had a fondness for playing outlaw. "Wild Bill" Hickok, the famed frontier marshal, had flourished in Abilene itself, and they had a fine time enacting his battles with cattle rustlers, using sticks as pistols.

Although their mother was not happy to see them "shooting" away at each other, this game troubled her less than another they liked even better. During

A snapshot of young Dwight (right) with his friends in Abilene. He appears to have surrendered.

and after the Spanish-American War of 1898, they would charge about the side yard, brandishing "rifles" and shouting as blood-thirstily as they could: "Remember the *Maine!*" That could bring tears to their mother's eyes.

For Mrs. Eisenhower was fervently religious and belonged to a sect, known as the River Brethren, which considered war the worst evil afflicting mankind. Because he loved his mother so much, Dwight never thought as a boy of becoming a soldier. The fact that he joined the Army—and went on to be one of the great generals in American history—was almost an accident.

During high school Dwight put most of his energy into playing football and baseball, though he came out better than average at classwork too. After gradua-

tion he spent another year in Abilene, working with his father at the dairy. Arthur had already gone off to Kansas City, and was on his way to a successful career as a banker. Edgar wanted to be a lawyer and had enrolled in college. Even the younger boys were aiming more or less directly for the professions in which they would later do well—Roy as a pharmacist, Earl as an electrical engineer and Milton as a government official and college president.

But although Dwight definitely wanted to go to college, he was not set on any particular career. So he had made a deal with Edgar. Dwight would work a few years to help Ed through college—then Ed would do the same for him. By the time his own turn came, he hoped he would have a clearer idea of what he wanted to study.

It was an Abilene friend who put him on the path to fame. The friend was a year or two younger than Dwight, and not much of a math student. Because he was so eager to become a sailor, he was desperately boning up in order to pass the Annapolis entrance exam. Dwight had never had any particular trouble with math or any other subject —especially history, which he liked best of all. He was helping the would-be admiral when suddenly the thought struck him: why not take the Annapolis exam himself?

It turned out there was a sound answer. By the time he could be admitted, if he scored high enough on the test, he would have passed his twentieth birthday, and the Naval Academy accepted no entrants that old. But before he discovered this fact, he had already taken the test. And merely in order to give himself the benefit of every possible opportunity, he had indicated that he wanted to be considered for West Point too.

Thus it came about that Cadet Dwight D. Eisenhower entered the United States Military Academy in September of 1911, while his friend went to Annapolis.

Dwight's mother had wept, as he had known she would. But her religion not only abhorred war; it also taught that every creature had the right to go his own way. Dwight himself felt that the chance for a good education could not be turned down, and his father agreed. But Mrs. Eisenhower's strong influence on her third son was by no means ended. In the years to come, Dwight showed in many ways that even as a soldier, he hated war. Writing about the advance of American troops into Germany during World War II, he said: "My purpose was to bring the whole bloody business to an end."

At West Point, Cadet Eisenhower made a good if not outstanding record, especially when it came to football; he won a place on the Army team as a half-back and played hard till a knee injury benched him. What he did best, though, was win friends. Somehow almost all of those who came in contact with him marked him down as a solid sort of person, someone who could be trusted.

He came out slightly above average in his marks, but nobody thought he was brilliant. Nor did he have the flash and dash of some classmates who, if the opportunity arose, might turn into battle heroes. It was mainly Ike's broad grin that people remembered, and his gift for getting on easily with almost everybody. These, plus his willingness to work hard, seemed to promise that he might expect a modest success in his Army career.

During the years of routine duty that followed graduation, Lieutenant Eisenhower married Miss Mamie Doud of Denver. At Army posts in various parts of the country, the couple made more friends. Although Ike was eager to go overseas during the First World War, he was assigned instead to various commands in this country, including a tank-corps training center in Pennsylvania.

Indeed it was not until seven years after the war, when he was sent to take a course at the Army's Command and General Staff School at Fort Leavenworth in 1925, that he showed he might be more than merely capable. This school, in effect, was the testing ground for future generals. The most complex problems of military tactics were taken up here, and for the first time Ike Eisenhower was challenged to put his mind to work as hard as it could; he came out first in his class.

Even so, the next fifteen years brought him no startling promotions. In the peacetime Army, seniority was the key to promotion and there were many capable officers ahead of him in length of service. By the spring of 1941, he had advanced in rank only to lieutenant colonel.

For four years, he had been in the Philippine Islands as senior military assistant to General Douglas MacArthur. Their assignment was to build and train a Filipino fighting force strong enough to counter possible aggression by the Japanese. On returning home, Lieutenant Colonel Eisenhower found the whole United States Army in a frenzy of expansion, spurred by the threat of American involvement in Europe's war as well. The sky over London was already red with flames from the fires started by German bombs.

Eisenhower took up his new assignment—the planning of training exercises in Louisiana. His feat of whipping raw recruits into an effective combat team, as demonstrated in a series of sham battles, brought high praise from his superiors and promotion. Then shortly after the attack on Pearl Harbor in December 1941, his telephone rang.

"Is that you, Ike?" the voice on the other end inquired.

"Yes."

"The Chief says for you to hop a plane and get up here right away. Tell your boss that formal orders will come through later."

Eisenhower had recognized the voice immediately as belonging to one of his old friends, now serving as aide to the Army's Chief of Staff, General George C. Marshall. "The Chief" was Marshall himself. Wasting no time, Ike left for Washington.

Presenting himself at the War Department, he was ushered into General Marshall's office at once. The two men had met briefly several times, but the opportunities for conversation had been limited and they hardly knew each other. More different personalities would have been hard to imagine; Marshall had the restrained and formal manner of a Virginia gentleman, Eisenhower the open, affable air he had brought to West Point from the Kansas prairie. But over the years, they both had become expert at the science of warfare, and their country stood in desperate need of such knowledge.

For twenty minutes, Marshall crisply outlined the strategic situation facing the United States on far-flung Pacific battlefronts, and then he posed a question:

"What should be our general line of action?"

Eisenhower reflected an instant, then answered: "Give me a few hours."

A few hours later, after carefully reviewing various possibilities in his mind, he faced Marshall once more and said:

"General, it will be a long time before major reinforcements can go to the Philippines, longer than any garrison can hold out with driblet assistance, if the enemy commits major forces to their reduction. But we must do everything for them that is humanly possible."

171

And he went on to explain his proposed strategy in detail.

"I agree with you," General Marshall said. Impressed with Ike's grasp of strategy, Marshall appointed Eisenhower as his principal assistant, with the rank of major general. In Congress, there was some curiosity about why an officer with no outward claim to special competence had been promoted ahead of a few dozen higher up on the seniority list. But within the Army, heads nodded sagely and there were murmurs: "Marshall picked a good man."

It was not long before other people began to be impressed by Dwight Eisenhower. For six of the darkest months in American history—months during which our Navy staggered back from the blow struck at Pearl Harbor and General MacArthur was forced to abandon the Philippines and the nation's industrial machine was laboriously changing over to producing war equipment—Major General Eisenhower worked within the War Department helping to decide top-secret questions of policy.

Which commanders in the field should get the first reinforcements? Should priority go to building oil tankers or pipe lines? What was the best role for our air arm? Eisenhower's grasp of the essentials in each case increasingly impressed General Marshall.

Thus in the early summer of 1942, when Marshall needed a reliable firsthand report about conditions in England, he sent Ike overseas. When the report came in, tersely outlining the military situation there and suggesting steps to be taken, including the appointment of a unified American command for Europe,

Winston Churchill with Dwight D. Eisenhower.

Marshall did not hesitate. "I'm giving you the job," he told Eisenhower.

First as the top American officer in England, then as supreme commander of the mightiest international military force ever assembled, Dwight D. Eisenhower became one of the world's great heroes.

He demonstrated for the first time that cockneys from the slums of London, GIs from Oregon and Texas and New York, Canadians, Norwegians and Frenchmen—men serving under many separate flags but united in their hatred for Hitler—could all be forged into an efficient fighting team.

Past efforts at combined military operations had sometimes succeeded, but had always been accompanied by bickering and worse among the so-called partners. Petty questions of which general or which regiment should lead the way, or set the master strategy, had weakened the Allied effort in the First World War.

Without any doubt, the grand alliance formed by President Franklin D. Roosevelt, British Prime Minister Winston Churchill and Russian Premier Josef Stalin, along with the heads of many smaller states, produced the basic unity in World War II. And the combined planning staffs deserved credit for formulating specific campaigns.

But the captain of the team when it took to the field was General Eisenhower —and the free world could not have been luckier.

The same broad grin that had made friends in Abilene and West Point made more friends in London. If any American officer complained about an English colleague, Eisenhower had a stock answer: "Get on with the British, or get out!" In his own dealings with the English, he had no trouble. When they gave him the key to the city of London in a ceremony some time later, he offered his explanation for the easy comradeship:

"I am not a native of this land," he said. "I come from the very heart of America. . . . But—a fact important for both of us to remember—neither London nor Abilene, sisters under the skin, will sell liberty for mere existence."

Eisenhower became a symbol of Allied unity, but he provided more than symbolic leadership. Few men have ever borne as much responsibility for making decisions directly affecting millions of lives as he assumed in 1942, 1943 and 1944.

When the Anglo-American summit leadership decided to start its offense against the Germans by invading North Africa, Eisenhower commanded that operation. He led the Allied drives in Sicily and Italy, too. Although the grand strategy was set at secret conferences of Allied leaders, he had to decide on the spot if weather conditions warranted changes in plans.

He also had to take on countless other problems. During the Italian campaign, for instance, he received word that the enemy had planted dangerous mines in the harbor selected as the destination for a British battle fleet carrying a division of soldiers. He had to risk a serious strain on Anglo-American unity by ordering the British to proceed into the perilous waters.

With the frankness that came naturally to him, Eisenhower told the British admiral who was serving under his command what might be expected in Taranto harbor. But by showing that his concern for the lives of Englishmen was no less than his concern for Americans, the Supreme Commander won more than mere cooperation. "Sir," said the British admiral, "His Majesty's fleet is here to go wherever you may send it!"

Afterward, Eisenhower wrote in his own account of the war: "The terrific pressure under which we worked is hard to appreciate now."

While the grim fighting was going on, that pressure never relented. To a foot soldier under artillery fire, a general's problems might seem comparatively simple. But the infantryman only has to save his own life, and possibly those of some of his company; General Eisenhower had on his shoulders the responsibility for whole armies.

Unquestionably, the biggest single decision he had to make—and possibly the most important decision any man has had to make on his own—involved the timing of the Allied invasion of France in the spring of 1944. Operation Overlord, its code name, had been planned down to the finest detail. Virtually all of southern England had become a vast embarkation camp; the complexities of organizing men, supplies and landing boats almost defied description. All was in readiness for the signal from General Eisenhower.

Then the weather unexpectedly worsened. Low clouds, high winds and formidable waves on the English Channel were predicted for the night of June 4. Eisenhower postponed the whole enormous undertaking till the next night.

On the afternoon of June 5, conditions had not improved much. But further delay would bring less favorable tides. Another postponement might mean the loss of a full month, conceivably even the loss of the war.

"I went to my tent alone and sat down to think," Eisenhower wrote later.

The decision had to be his alone, and he made it. "OK, we'll go," he said.

His courageous decision changed the course of world history. After successfully establishing beachheads in France on June 6, the Allied forces fought their way inland. Less than three months later, on August 25, Paris was liberated. By the following spring, Allied armies had overrun Germany itself—and the war in Europe was over.

After relieving General Marshall as Chief of Staff, Eisenhower in the late 1940's thought the time had come for him to try life as a private citizen, working a little less than sixteen hours a day. His only son, a recent West Point graduate, had given him several grandchildren. He craved some leisure to enjoy watching them grow up, and to play all the golf he had never been able to fit in, to challenge old friends to beat him at bridge or poker.

The post of president of Columbia University was offered to him—and he

"Full victory" is the order of the day as U.S. paratroopers prepare to invade Europe on D-Day.

accepted it. But President Harry Truman had other plans for him. Late in 1950, Eisenhower put on his uniform again to become commander of the military arm of the North American Treaty Organization, with headquarters outside of Paris.

From this assignment, the American people as a whole retired him. By an overwhelming vote, they chose Dwight D. Eisenhower as their President in 1952, and then again four years later. They proved how much they loved and trusted the former warrior with the engaging grin by ignoring ordinary political considerations. Political experts marveled at the number of Democrats who voted for this Republican candidate.

But politics had never been his main consideration, and he did not change in this respect during his years in the White House. Keeping the peace was his object, and by his efforts to ward off new conflicts while he was the nation's chief executive, President Eisenhower once more earned the supreme gratitude of his countrymen. After retiring to the farm he had bought in Pennsylvania, he told an interviewer that his own personal hero was George Washington. Eisenhower was far too modest to compare himself with the nation's first President. But millions of others would never forget that Eisenhower, too, had served the United States courageously, in war and in peace.

For Further Reading

Our basic research tool was contemporary accounts in the pages of *The New York Times*. Among our book sources, we recommend the following for those who want to know more about the careers of the heroes we have discussed:

ANDERSON

Anderson, Marian. *My Lord, What a Morning!* Viking, 1956.

BOURKE-WHITE

Bourke-White, Margaret. *Portrait of Myself.* Simon and Schuster, 1963.

BYRD

Byrd, Richard E. *Skyward.* Putnam, 1928.

Byrd, Richard E. *Discovery.* Putnam, 1935.

CATT

Peck, Mary Gray. *Carrie Chapman Catt.* Wilson, 1944.

Sinclair, Andrew. *The Better Half.* Harper, 1965.

DONOVAN

Alcorn, Robert Haydon. *No Banners, No Bands.* McKay, 1965.

Editors of the *Army Times. Modern American Secret Agents.* Dodd, Mead, 1966.

Lovell, Stanley. *Of Spies and Stratagems.* Prentice-Hall, 1963.

EARHART

Goerner, Fred. *The Search for Amelia Earhart.* Doubleday, 1966.

EISENHOWER

Davis, Kenneth S. *Soldier of Democracy.* Doubleday, 1945.

Eisenhower, Dwight D. *Crusade in Europe.* Doubleday, 1948.

Gunther, John. *Eisenhower, the Man and the Symbol.* Harper, 1952.

GODDARD

Goddard, Robert H. *Rockets.* American Rocket Society, 1946.

Goddard, Robert H. *Rocket Development.* Prentice-Hall, 1961.

Lehman, Milton. *This High Man.* Farrar, Straus, 1963.

KELLER

Harrity, Richard, and Martin, Ralph G. *The Three Lives of Helen Keller.* Doubleday, 1962.

Keller, Helen. *The Story of My Life.* Doubleday, 1954.

KENNEDY

Donovan, Robert. *PT 109.* McGraw-Hill, 1961.

Faber, Harold, editor. *The Kennedy Years.* Viking, 1964.

Whalen, Richard. *The Founding Father.* New American Library, 1964.

KING

King, Martin Luther. *Stride Toward Freedom.* Harper, 1958.

LINDBERGH

Lindbergh, Charles A. *The Spirit of St. Louis.* Scribner, 1953.

MAC ARTHUR

MacArthur, Douglas. *Reminiscences.* McGraw-Hill, 1964.

MURPHY

Murphy, Audie. *To Hell and Back.* Holt, 1949.

MURROW

Murrow, Edward R. *This Is London.* Simon and Schuster, 1941.

PYLE

Pyle, Ernie. *Here Is Your War.* Holt, 1943.

Pyle, Ernie. *Brave Men.* Holt, 1944.

Pyle, Ernie. *Last Chapter.* Holt, 1946.

ROOSEVELT

Freidel, Frank. *Franklin D. Roosevelt, the Apprenticeship.* Little-Brown, 1952.

Freidel, Frank. *Franklin D. Roosevelt, the Ordeal.* Little-Brown, 1954.

Freidel, Frank. *Franklin D. Roosevelt, the Triumph.* Little-Brown, 1956.

Roosevelt, Sara Delano, as told to Isabel Leighton and Gabriele Forbush. *My Boy Franklin.* Long and Smith, 1933.

SALK

Carter, Richard. *Breakthrough: The Saga of Jonas Salk.* Trident, 1966.

Williams, Greer. *Virus Hunters.* Knopf, 1959.

SEAGRAVE

Seagrave, Gordon. *The Life of a Burma Surgeon.* Norton, 1961.

SHEPARD

Carpenter, M. Scott, et al. *We Seven.* Simon and Schuster, 1962.

National Aeronautics and Space Administration. *Results of Conference of the First U.S. Manned Suborbital Space Flight.* Government Printing Office, 1961.

ABOUT THE AUTHORS

Doris Faber's thirteen books for young readers include biographies of Robert Frost, Clarence Darrow, Enrico Fermi, Horace Greeley, John Jay, and Pocahontas. She is also the author of *The Wonderful Tumble of Timothy Smith* (Knopf) and *Behind the Headlines: The Story of Newspapers* (Pantheon). For eight years she was a reporter for *The New York Times.* Married to Harold Faber, she retired from the *Times* to raise their two daughters.

Harold Faber, Editorial Director of *The New York Times* Book and Educational Division, was formerly Day National News Editor of the *Times.* He served in the Army during World War II, and was wounded as a combat correspondent in Korea. The best seller *The Kennedy Years* was prepared under his editorial direction. He is the author of a biography of George C. Marshall for young readers.

The Fabers and their daughters live in Pleasantville, N. Y.

Index

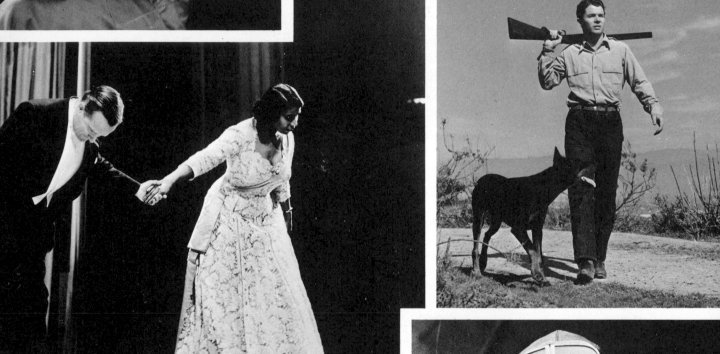